BUILDING THE BBC

A RETURN TO FORM

CONTENTS

Foreword 4

Introduction 6

Chapter 1/Seeing the light 9

Chapter 2/Broadcasting House 1932 19

Chapter 3/The learning curve 33

Chapter 4/The new Broadcasting House 47

Chapter 5/Television Centre 73

Chapter 6/White City 87

Chapter 7/Pacific Quay 107

Chapter 8/The heart of the community 123

Chapter 9/Public art 135

Credits/Acknowledgements 155

FOREWORD

To give tangible, architectural, expression to an ideal is a fascinating and daunting challenge. And when that ideal embraces powerful, yet essentially abstract, actions such as the gathering and dissemination of news, and has at its core the mission to inform, inspire, educate and entertain the public, then the challenge to the architect is truly awe-inspiring.

How can the action of broadcasting to the nation be expressed when it is an enterprise loaded with such powerful political and social implications? Television and radio broadcasters can make and amend public perceptions, they can create and break trends, they can give the nation a voice and, ominously, can virtually tell it what to think and say. Broadcasting is an immensely powerful tool in the creation, manipulation and expression of public opinion in all fields and so has to be used, indeed has to be seen by the public to be used, with great care, consideration and openness. And when the broadcaster is a public corporation – supported by a licence fee paid by all who watch television – then openness of operation becomes more than just a nicety. It becomes a paramount concern, an almost sacred obligation.

Since the BBC received its Royal Charter in 1926 generations of architects have wrestled with the problem of providing it with offices and studios that both fulfil the technical demands of broadcasting a wide range of subjects and that express the significance of the operation. Architectural symbolism is significant but what exactly should be symbolised? The objective way in which information is gathered and transmitted, the physics and science of broadcasting or the way in which broadcasting can unite, bond, inform and educate the nation? What is fascinating are the varied ways in which architects and BBC executives have, during the last 70 years or so, approached the complex issue of giving physical expression to the activities of the Corporation.

Building the BBC tells the story of the BBC's role as patron of architecture and the arts – a role that it has, at times, embraced wholeheartedly and effectively but in which it has also, at several critical moments, failed lamentably. The architectural consequences of these highs and lows make a gripping story. The first great act of patronage came in 1932, during the reign of the BBC's first and great General Manager John Reith, with the completion of Broadcasting House in Portland Place. Here the symbolism is clear. A monumental public building – in the solid stripped classical language of the time – that announced the BBC as a new and formidable power in the land; already established, and part of the cultural establishment, after less than 10 years of existence.

There were few major architectural successes during the following decades (the 1950s Television Centre in Shepherd's Bush is one), and many architectural lows. In general the BBC has preferred to keep a discreet profile architecturally, commissioning or occupying unexceptional and utilitarian structures. The fact that by 2001 it occupied no less than 520 properties across Britain, with only a handful being in any sense architecturally memorable, suggests very strongly that in the BBC architectural patronage – or perhaps procurement would be a better word – was firmly in the grip of those who lacked vision or courage. But, among its many roles, the BBC is one of the great patrons of the arts in Britain. It commissions drama, it nurtures actors and a whole range of original and creative talent, ranging from directors and writers to designers and historians, and has a responsibility to at least attempt to commission architecture of the highest quality.

For the moment at least things have changed. The BBC has found its nerve again and risen to the responsibility of its role as national champion and patron of the arts. It is attempting to lead by example and in the last three years has commissioned a series of major buildings that suggest an artistic renaissance is taking place within the Corporation and that the quest for architectural excellence is, at the very least, an issue and once again an ideal to aim for. Achieved through international competitions, these buildings have been designed by some of the most admired and able architects in the country. All suggest a very modern image for the BBC in which current technologies of construction are expressed and fused with the equally futuristic, and ever evolving, technologies of 21st century broadcasting. But these buildings also have another thing in common. The watch-word now is openness – and all the structures envisage the maximum involvement of the public in the process, the theatre, and certainly in the architecture, of broadcasting. They imply, quite simply, that broadcasting should be, literally as well as notionally, transparent. Walls of glass abound, public galleries and streets penetrate to the hearts of the schemes. The message is clear; the public should see, share and enjoy what it is paying for. This book, despite its accounts of the gloomy years, makes very encouraging reading.

Dan Cruickshank
Architectural historian and broadcaster.

INTRODUCTION

More than virtual reality

Within the next couple of years this will be the shape of the BBC: BBC News will be transmitted to millions of television viewers across the globe against a backdrop of the largest, purpose-designed newsroom in the world. This magnificent, day-lit space will frame All Souls Church, one of London's architectural jewels. Shoppers might be jostling to see which celebrity is turning on the Christmas Lights, not from the old spot in Oxford Circus but from an exceptional vantage point in London's newest public square, right next to Broadcasting House with a fantastic view down the entire length of Regent Street.

Further north, the low winter sun will be reflecting in the shimmering glass of BBC Scotland's new building alongside the River Clyde. Like a phoenix rising from the ashes, the translucent building will represent a new confidence in this previously forgotten district of Glasgow, contributing to the renaissance of the city's new media and cultural quarter.

At the new White City Music Centre, in west London, audiences will mingle in the spatially dynamic foyers before a performance by the BBC Symphony Orchestra. Outside, hundreds of BBC staff, local workers and residents will move through the beautifully lit, landscaped streets and open spaces, doing some shopping on their way home. White City, a previously neglected area of London, will have become the place to be. New offices, shops, flats and houses will cluster around the recently occupied BBC offices and production offices, and the fondly refurbished BBC Television Centre. Across the road, a forest of cranes will indicate the birth of one of London's newest mixed-use neighbourhoods next to White City's new, spacious underground station.

Is this for real? And, if so, why has the BBC's image and its commitment to architecture changed so radically? *Building the BBC* describes a journey of enlightened patronage. It is also a tale of commercial decision making that has spawned a profound change in the Corporation's spatial culture. As a fellow traveller, I have seen the BBC transform itself in the space of a few years from a frankly shoddy property owner into a modern public client. So much so that it was selected as No 1 'Client of the Year' by the RIBA Journal in 2002, winning the design profession's Oscar.

The BBC has not been driven purely by its prodigious cultural appetite. It reflects the Corporation's business plan to respond to the fast-changing world of media. It recognises that those outdated, poorly maintained buildings spread across Britain no longer satisfy the demands of the BBC's sophisticated producers and consumers, nor do they stand up to the high standards offered by the competition. It reflects a commitment to the realisation of its assets through the consolidation of its property portfolio in new landmark buildings that will serve the Corporation well into the 21st century.

In 2000 the BBC's senior executives led the way for a new policy of ownership, procurement and design. Instead of retrofitting its stock of ageing buildings, the Corporation decided to invest in a new generation of purpose-designed buildings. The process of this investment is a radical as the product. A major private-sector developer, Land Securities Trillium, has been contracted to fund, build and manage all BBC property for 30 years. This innovative approach has transferred the risk of building and running buildings to the private sector, allowing the BBC to concentrate on what it does best. While it is too soon to draw conclusions, the impact on design quality is already well established.

The BBC jumped at the prospect of using design competitions to procure the best architects. Two years ago I joined BBC senior executives and advisers in visits to half-completed buildings in Berlin, Delft, Rotterdam, Cambridge and Henley-on-Thames in their quest to find the right designers. They marvelled at many of the designs. They grilled the clients on cost, maintenance and the architects' ability to deliver. They put some of Europe's leading architects through their paces with a series of workshops to test their understanding of the BBC's idiosyncratic working culture. Finally, though, it was the quality of the architecture that won the day.

Allies & Morrison's practical and urbane approach has turned what could have been an office fortress into an open working community for over 5,000 people in White City, with buildings of elegance and economy, and generous public and communal spaces. The Music Centre, which will be designed by one of five world-famous architects, will add to the public ethos of this emerging neighbourhood. David Chipperfield's immaculately detailed building, with its dramatic stepped atrium rising the whole length of BBC Scotland's headquarters in Glasgow, will transform the way people work and interact, inside and outside the building. MacCormac Jamieson Prichard's curved addition to Broadcasting House brings together the BBC World Service, all the domestic radio stations and all news services under one roof. The public will walk through the building at ground level, giving the BBC a much-needed civic presence in central

London with an innovative glass and stone screen that amplifies transparency between the building and the city.

While the architectural language and style of each building is different, the themes of engagement are constant. The projects are a physical incarnation of the BBC's brief to introduce innovative working practices – less hierarchy, more interaction and greater transparency. But it is the connection to the city that reflects a true shift in paradigm. The desire to expose the BBC 'at work', to invite people in and to play a far more public role than in the past, has contributed to the creation of more open buildings that have strong expressive potential.

So, in a few years' time, as we walk through these new buildings we will be able to judge for ourselves whether the gamble has paid off. I suspect it will. I will be surprised if all the architects do not scoop major design awards for their buildings soon after completion. More awards will be showered on the Music Centre, when the winning scheme of the next exciting competition is built. And perhaps there will be accolades for BBC buildings in Birmingham, Leicester, Nottingham and elsewhere. These awards will be well deserved, both by the architects and by the BBC, their enlightened client.

Ricky Burdett
Director, LSE Cities Programme,
and architectural adviser to the BBC.

1

SEEING THE LIGHT

1 A temporary light work for BBC Broadcasting House by artist David Ward. Illuminated from dusk until dawn each night from 12 December 2002 to 5 January 2003. Image © 2003 Photographer Rod Dorling.

'Work stops at sunset.
Darkness falls over the building site.
The sky is filled with stars.
"There is the blueprint" they say'
Italo Calvino: *Invisible Cities*.

SEEING THE LIGHT

When Val Myer's bold design for Broadcasting House was completed in 1932 broadcasters were promised the use of 'a small apartment necessary for news' among the 20 studios. Little could the architect or his client have foreseen the voracious appetite for news and the explosive development in broadcast technology that would result in the creation of the world's largest newsroom on the same site 75 years later.

The redevelopment of Broadcasting House (BH) by MacCormac Jamieson Prichard Architects, set for completion in 2007, is just one of many BBC architectural projects currently underway. After decades of indecision, the Corporation is consolidating its nationwide operations within well-designed, efficiently run buildings equipped for digital radio and television and online operations. More importantly for licence fee payers, these buildings will allow the public to walk through the heart of the organisation, past recording studios and newsrooms and into public spaces that will welcome us and demand our active participation.

During the 1990s, independent broadcasters throughout Europe began to recognise the importance of giving their organisations a public face. In London Richard Rogers was commissioned to design a headquarters for Channel 4 near Victoria. The striking aluminium-clad building was finished in 1994. That was after his friend and rival, Norman Foster, had designed the sleek new ITN headquarters in Gray's Inn Road, with its full-height atrium soaring through the building's 10 storeys. In 1992, New York architect Richard Meier was brought to Paris to create an identity in clear, translucent and opaque glass for Canal+. These projects all took shape during a period in which Britain's premier broadcaster built very little of architectural interest. The 1970s and 1980s were equally dismal. In 2001 the number of BBC properties across the UK was estimated at an astonishing 520. Most of these offices and studios have remained invisible due to their unpropitious locations or their inefficient, unfashionable architecture.

In contrast to this inauspicious legacy, the new projects – particularly the flagship buildings in London, Broadcasting House and White City, and Pacific Quay in Glasgow – look certain to attract even more attention than the revolutionary Broadcasting House did in 1932. In August of that year an issue of *The Architectural Review* was dedicated to the new building in Portland Place by Lieutenant-Colonel G Val Myer and Marmaduke T Tudsbery, the BBC's Civil Engineer. The

1

2

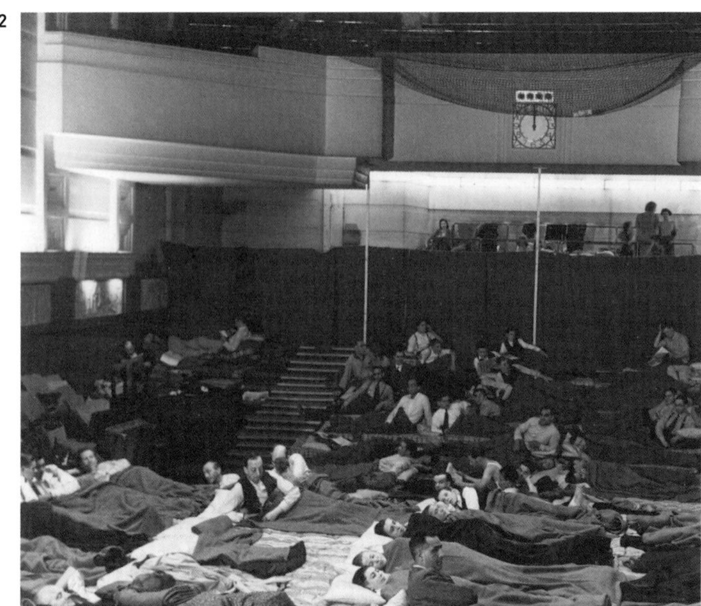

3

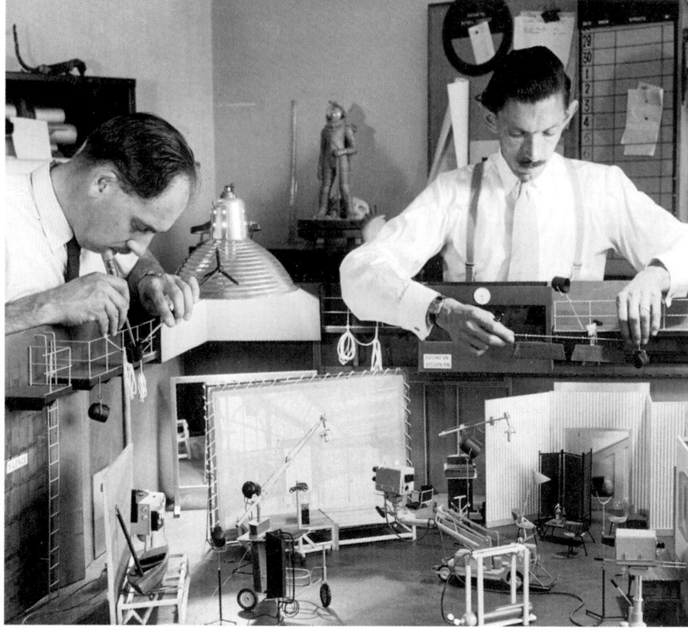

magazine called it 'a new Tower of London. On the covers of magazines, on films, in catalogues, in guide books, in all the many means of publicity the new BBC building, its studios, its gadgets, its engineering devices, will appear ... [it becomes] a trade-mark for Broadcasting ... something more than a mere block of offices, enclosing a sound factory; like the Tower of London, it becomes a national monument.' Like the Tower, the building had its central *donjon*, the studios, surrounded by an outer ring of defences, the public and service ways. Here was a building that caught the imagination and attempted – largely successfully – to encapsulate the vision of the British Broadcasting Corporation in the early days of radio.

There was another notable architectural success for the BBC before the vacuum of the 1970s, 1980s and 1990s, in the shape of Television Centre in London's Shepherd's Bush. The confident design was conceived on an envelope by architect Graham Dawbarn in the 1950s. It became, and has remained, one of the best-designed television production houses in the world. Its question mark form was inspired, with the studios on the ground floor and a ring road wrapped around it to allow easy access for equipment through double-height doors. Like Broadcasting House, it embraced the age in which it was built. Both buildings were forward-looking in their design and were designed at a time when huge leaps were being made in terms of technology and programme output (see chapters 2 and 5). Broadcasting House and Television Centre reflected the excitement and glamour of broadcasting in the 1930s and 1960s and are the only two buildings

2 Staff sleeping on mattresses in the Concert Hall of Broadcasting House during the Second World War, 1940.

3 A model studio built for display at the 1955 National Radio and Television Exhibition to demonstrate some of the effects used in television production.

4 Richard Dimbleby, David Butler and Robert McKenzie announcing the results of the 1959 General Election from Studio G, Lime Grove.

5 Ann Ross and Valerie Pitts in Studio H, Lime Grove, where all the live pictures for the EBU colour demonstrations originated.

4

5

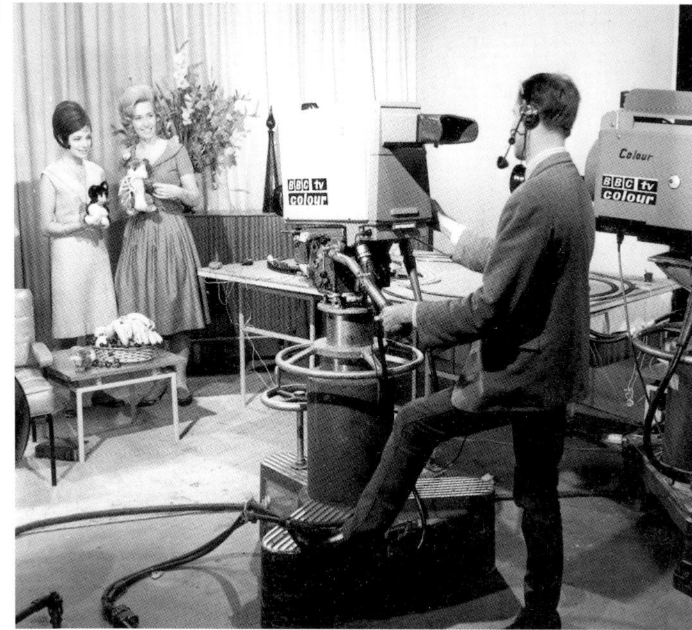

that most of the general public can cite as BBC property today, with the possible exception of Birmingham's Pebble Mill. Bush House, although occupied by the BBC, is not owned by the Corporation.

After the success of Television Centre came three decades in which spending on maintaining existing buildings and investment in new architecture started to fall away. Buildings were no longer considered as strategic assets and became mere commodities. BBC employees were forced to develop a Dunkirk spirit to their workplace. Roly Keating, Controller of BBC4, describes Lime Grove, acquired as temporary television studios in the early 1950s but used until 1991, as 'chaotic, rambling'.

He adds: 'There were lots of times when we had to sprint through rain to deliver tapes. But it was a stimulus to creativity and passion, to going the extra mile. Working there was a totally memorable, textured, alive experience despite [the offices and studios] being the opposite of a perfect architectural space. People are not being perverse when they express that. It's a profound feeling which can't be engineered. But you need to understand what it means.'

This is not to say that Keating is dragging his feet over the new buildings. Indeed, he is one of the advocates of a more intelligent and imaginative approach to commissioning architecture. His concern is that architects should be 'sympathetic not prescriptive' when designing buildings that will inevitably need to grow and adapt with the advent of new technology and developments in programme making. 'They need to create a spirit that works. That is an art, not a science.'

So what was the catalyst for the construction boom in London and Glasgow, as well as other regional buildings in cities such as Birmingham, Norwich, Leeds, Leicester and Hull, and why tackle three major projects simultaneously? Was it a change of captaincy of the great ship that was in danger of running aground in Portland Place? Was it because of a chronic and immediate need for more space to accommodate more sophisticated technology and growing numbers of staff in the digital age? Or was it simply a campaign to show the public where Auntie hangs out? The answer is all of the above; the logical culmination of what was initially called the '2020 Vision', a document – and phrase – very much associated with John Birt and run by Tony Hall, then head of News.

6

7

John Smith, the BBC's Director, Finance, Property and Business Affairs, has been at the heart of the building programme. The desire for 'decent quality architecture across the whole estate' is, he says, the prime motivation for the change in property strategy. Although the seeds were sown in Birt's era, it is only in the last few years that practical steps have been taken to make much of the blue-sky thinking a reality. 'The arrival of Greg Dyke as Director-General defined a new "can-do" mentality amongst BBC management. He elevated the status of property to the BBC's top executive level, putting architecture once again at the heart of the BBC's strategy.' Extensions that were boring, and even bad, had been annexed to Broadcasting House and Television Centre. Many of the buildings housing the 40 local radio stations had been built with function as the only criteria.

Smith describes the nadir of this low-quality period as the White City building in London W12. A poll of BBC personnel in 2000 revealed it as the most hated building of the estate. 'It would be a mistake to blame the architect; the brief and the budget came from a BBC that had lost its architectural way. This would have continued had there not been change at the top', says Smith. 'They were about to proceed with more faceless building at Egton House [home of Radio 1] and 16 Langham Street, sites which are key, sitting alongside All Souls church and Broadcasting House. I just said no. We had to do something.'

Smith and his colleagues were aware that the BBC's properties were being ignored as assets and he was convinced that a way could be found to use their presence, location and architecture 'to welcome in the licence paying public. Buildings should be crucial to our whole strategy, not incidental to it.' Perhaps surprisingly for a financial director, Smith promoted the idea that although money and availability were considerations, they were not the only ones. 'We had to find a way of getting into the heart of where all the people are. You've got to force yourself to think differently about finding the space and perhaps challenge the notion that it is imperative to own every site. We looked at some of the great buildings – both old and new – in city centres and found ways in which we could secure space within them. Hence Mailbox in Birmingham and the Forum in Norwich.'

In the late 1990s, Smith took a group to the CNN headquarters in Atlanta. 'We'd heard on

8

9

6+7 The Channel 4 headquarters in London's Horseferry Road near Victoria, was designed by the Richard Rogers Partnership. It was completed in 1994 and gave the channel a striking public image in line with its remit as a forward-thinking, independent broadcaster.

8+9 Foster Associates had set the standard with the new headquarters for ITN in Gray's Inn Road, completed in 1990. Its full-height atrium dominates the building's ten-storey interior.

the grapevine that they were making an effort to get thousands of people to come and see the heart of their operations. They'd built the CNN Center and bought enough land to ensure that the national indoor arena for Atlanta is on their site, and the only way you can get into it is by walking through the CNN Center ... all the escalators take you through the news operation and you're given a badge and a cap – it's like being sheep-dipped!' That trip led the BBC to think that its own news operation could be opened up to the public.

Smith also cites the public access to the Capital Radio café (since closed) in its headquarters as a way in which a building can be used as a strategic asset – the building is promoted over the airwaves and the programmes are promoted within the building, creating a virtuous circle. In stark contrast to Capital, our buildings aren't branded, we never invite people in when we're on air, but we're the nation's broadcaster and everyone pays for the privilege of watching and listening to our programmes. What's more, we are present in over 40 cities across the UK. The scope we have to open our buildings to the public is 10 times what it was for Capital.'

Before joining the BBC, Smith worked for the British Railways Property Board, one of the largest private landlords in Britain. He was there during the redevelopment of Broadgate. Stuart Lipton (of property developer Stanhope, and now chairman of the Commission for Architecture and the Built Environment, CABE) and Godfrey Bradman (of Rosehaugh) 'came to the board and proposed that Liverpool Street Station and Broadgate both needed redeveloping. They offered us many millions in cash and said they would completely rebuild the stations, ticket halls, tracks and signalling, in return for being allowed to build something they wanted above it. It was great. The railways got new infrastructure and some hard cash and gave to the private sector this huge new development. This idea of taking a public asset and giving up something to the private sector led to our decision to redevelop White City with a private sector developer.'

In 1999, Ian Robertson was brought on board as the BBC's Director, Property to run the process of finding a partner. 'The drivers for the private sector partnership were transfer of risk and the creation of valuable assets, along with the need to finance the projects and maintain a steady cash flow', explains Robertson. The 30-year deal with Land Securities Trillium, which includes the

12

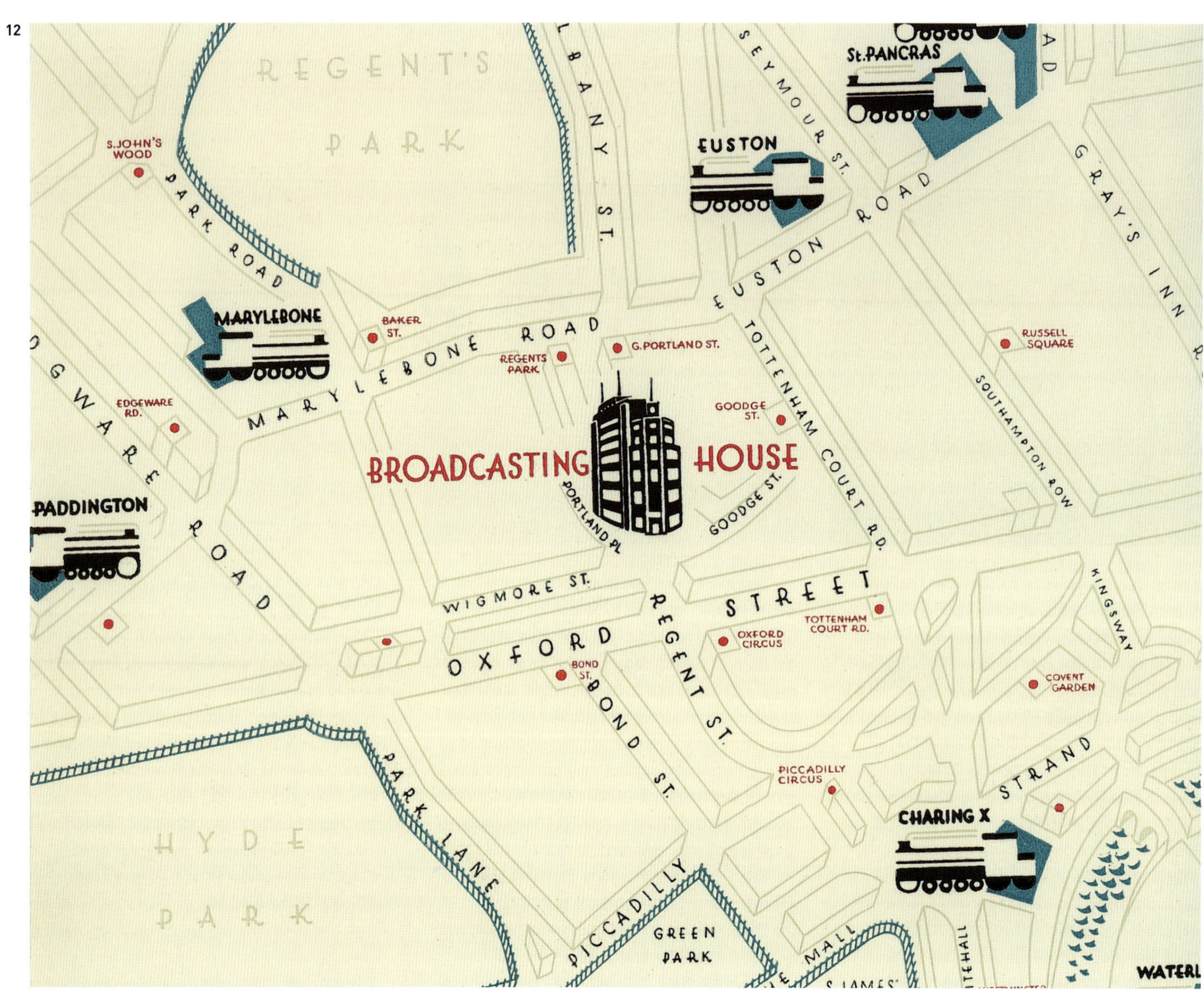

12 Map of London showing position of Broadcasting House. *Broadcasting House, The British Broadcasting Corporation, 1932.*

2

BROADCASTING HOUSE 1932

1 The public flooded in to Broadcasting House for live performances in the new Concert Hall. It was later to become the Radio Theatre.

BROADCASTING HOUSE 1932

The British Broadcasting Company, as it was first christened, was founded in 1922. It was created neither by a charter nor by journalists and aspiring broadcasters but by the manufacturers of the first radio sets.

Thanks to the work of 19th-century pioneers Guglielmo Marconi, the father of radio as we know it; Alexander Graham Bell, the inventor of speech transmission via the telephone; and Heinrich Hertz, the detector of radio waves, the Electrophone Company began transmitting programmes commercially over the telephone in 1894.

From about 1905 to 1920, the technology developed as a means of communication for the military and for use at sea, but programmes for the general public were severely limited. Manufacturers realised that if they were to sell their wares, there would have to be a broader enticement than, for example, Dame Nellie Melba singing Home Sweet Home from the world's first radio factory in Chelmsford.

The BBC's first General Manager was the 33-year-old John Reith, a First World War veteran from Kincardineshire who saw the BBC as first and foremost a public service. From the start Reith was passionate about using radio as a medium to disseminate ideas, to 'inform, educate and entertain'. The manufacturers embraced Reith's vision and soon agreed to turn the company over to the nation, with the agreement of the Government under Prime Minister Stanley Baldwin. Predictably, the only opposition came from the newspaper barons, who were concerned about the impact this new-fangled media would have on their circulation. But despite their protests a Royal Charter was granted and on 31 December 1926 the British Broadcasting Corporation was born.

In the late 1920s Germany was the only country to have a bespoke broadcasting facility, designed by Hans Poelzig on the outskirts of Berlin. The Rundfunkhaus was sited on the town boundary opposite what was known as the Radio Garden. This was part of the new exhibition quarter of Berlin, corresponding to London's White City, and it was seen as the edge of New Berlin. The smaller-scale Dutch Labour Party Broadcasting Station at Hilversum, by Snellebrand and Eibink (1932), and G Val Myer's Broadcasting House in central London signalled the birth of a new broadcasting age.

The BBC's first radio studio was on the top floor of Marconi House, on the Strand. The BBC had taken over Marconi's station 2LO ('2LO London Calling') in 1922, and the next year moved round the corner to Number 2 Savoy Hill (originally Savoy Mansions, a block of residential flats). Here, early contributors

1

2

3

including HG Wells and George Bernard Shaw were offered whisky and soda as they relaxed in the atmosphere of a gentlemen's club. Radio presenters were dressed in formal attire, complete with dicky bows, at all times. Radio drama flourished, weather forecasts and the Big Ben chimes were introduced and listeners could even follow coverage of the cricket. But the cosy environment, with its coal fires and oil paintings, soon became too cramped. The two studios expanded to nine, and before long the BBC was forced to look for a new home. And so began the journey that was to end with the glorious realisation in 1932 of Broadcasting House (BH), in London's Portland Place.

BBC Civil Engineer Marmaduke T Tudsbery was charged with finding a new building, or site, for the BBC in 1927. He considered several locations, including Dorchester House, an island site in Adelphi Terrace, the present site of Grosvenor House, the Grand Hotel in Trafalgar Square and sites in Exhibition Road and Haymarket. The freehold of the Langham Hotel, opposite the eventual site of Broadcasting House, was offered for £750,000, and the site of Bush House was considered as a possible development. At last, in the spring of 1927, Tudsbery happened upon the Portland Place site. The 20,000 square foot plot, home to four houses, was shaped like a flat-iron, 200 feet in length and 120 feet at the widest point. The owner, Lord Waring, was looking to sell the whole freehold, but the BBC could not afford to take it on and negotiations folded.

The following February Messrs Knight, Frank and Rutley informed Tudsbery that the site was to be let by Lord Waring to a financial syndicate that intended to develop it for residential purposes. However, they made clear to Tudsbery that, with sufficient financial and practical support from the BBC, the syndicate would be in a position to construct a building to suit its needs. Rent of six shillings per square foot was agreed and Robert Solomon, representing the syndicate, instructed its architect Val Myer to 'put before the BBC a perspective drawing and sketch plans for a building designed especially for the BBC's needs'.

Val Myer had started his own practice at the age of 19 and specialised in medium-sized houses. After the First World War he went to India to plan office buildings for the Bengal Government. This experience in modern office construction stood him in good stead when he was invalided home and eventually landed the Broadcasting House commission. Credit for the design and realisation of BH should also go to Tudsbery, who was charged with dealing

4

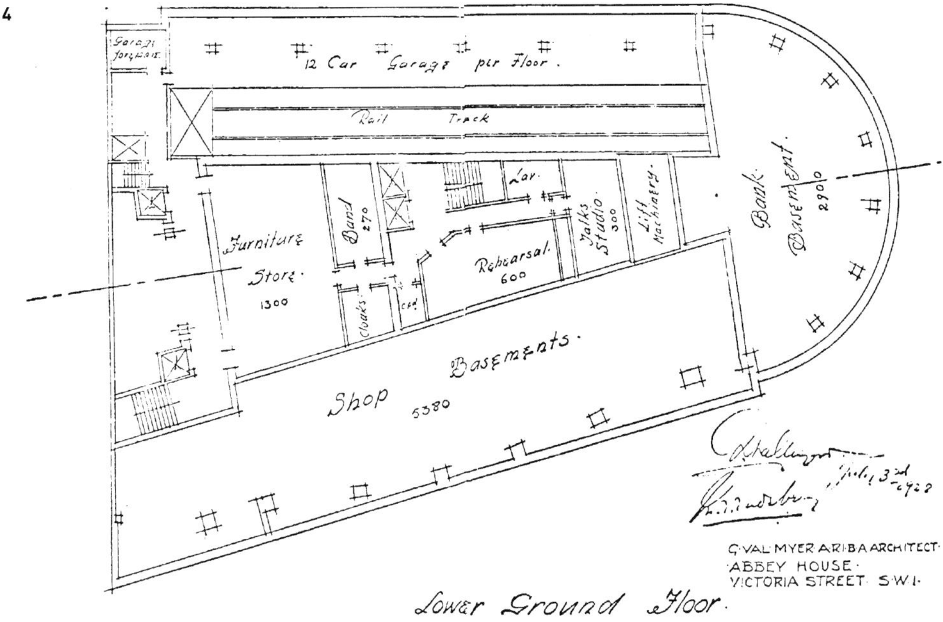

2 Drawing by Val Myer of the first scheme for BH, exhibited at the RA Summer Exhibition in 1927, and nicknamed the Top Hat.

3 Drawing of the long, curved west elevation fronting Portland Place. The studio tower is articulated by seven roundels above the office windows. The architectural language mixes modernism – in terms of the expression of technology – with conservatism, as reflected by the symmetry and formal composition.

4 Drawing of the lower ground floor of BH by Val Myer, dated July 3rd 1928. The occupation of the prow of the building by a bank was later abandoned in favour of a grand entrance.

with serious new technology as well as the BBC's board of directors.

The first scheme designed as a speculative venture for the syndicate by Val Myer (and illustrated by Fairey in a perspective view for the Royal Academy Summer Exhibition in 1927), was given the nickname the 'Top Hat' scheme, after the shape of the section. It was built in the spirit of the American skyscraper, which was cause for concern to some neighbours. Sir John Ellerman, who owned a property on the opposite site, was insistent that light to his property on the west of Langham Street should not be reduced. The design was therefore amended, but the combination of Scandinavian modernism and stripped-down classicism were to remain in the finished building.

The Architectural Review commented: 'The finished building ... represents the outcome of a struggle between moribund traditionalism and inventive modernism. Struggles of this kind are not as a rule conducive to good architecture, and still less to good decoration. But in this case, fortunately, the struggle ended in a victory which largely favoured the modernists ... The result is that, internally at least, the BBC has set an example comparable to that of the Underground and in pleasant contrast with that of such powerful and tasteless bodies as Imperial Chemical Industries and the Bank of England.'

The revised scheme went ahead on the understanding that the BBC would occupy 60,000 square feet of 'useful floor space' and a further 40,000 square feet would be sublet until required for further development. The parties also agreed that with the exception of the entrance, the lessors would develop the remainder of the ground floor and other floors for 'shops, banks, offices or other suitable purposes' – hence the shop-like windows looking onto Portland Place. In what now reads as a comic clause in the contract, certain tradesmen were barred from the site, including 'slaughterman ... sugar baker ... fellmonger ... common brewer ... beater of flax ... quasi-medical or quasi-surgical establishment, brothel or bagnio keeper'.

Of course at the time this was a serious business. The equivalent today would be the battle to keep chain coffee shops or high-street outlets from under the skirts of prestigious new arts complexes. The idea of having any trade on the site at all was that the Corporation would move into a building with room for future expansion. Val Myer wrote in a letter on 23 May 1928 that 'they now had to contemplate a building into which they could scarcely squeeze'. A plan to include a bank on the southern corner of the site was eventually dropped, and on

5

6

7

completion an ugly row of boarded-up shops with 'to let' signs fronted the street. The building was completed and occupied in 1931, and on 6 January 1936 the BBC purchased the freehold. No shops, other than the BBC's own, ever occupied the ground floor.

Sir John Reith was involved throughout the process. In a letter to Val Myer on 25 April 1929, he requested a meeting with the architect and governors 'so that there may be a general interchange of opinions on architectural embellishments and things of that order'. His main concern was about 'the plain front'. Val Myer wrote that, 'at an early date I realised that the site possessed a rare virtue in the long curve of the Western side, and so, in organising the proportion of my masses and the play of light and shade, I tried to make full use of the gracious horizontal lines which this curve suggested'.

Plans for the building were drawn up in which 'the guiding principle was to exploit to the utmost the peculiar advantages in shape and size of the offices and similar departments to which daylight is essential ... On the other hand, the studios and their suites, for which insulation from external noise is the first need, have been grouped in a vast central tower of heavy brickwork, ventilated by artificial means and protected from the streets by the complete outer layer of offices ... and insulated from the offices themselves by wide corridors and thick brick walls' (Taken from the report by Val Myer/Tudsbery, 3 July 1928). One of the more unusual studios was a chapel for the broadcast of the religious services, by architect Edward Maufe. It had a central recess which was lit to produce an effect of infinite distance. When religious programmes were being broadcast the shadow of a cross was projected onto the white background. For secular use the recess simply contained a vase of flowers.

In order to squeeze maximum usable space onto such a tight site, Val Myer had to banish ideas of inner courtyards or light wells. In the deep interior spaces, artificially lit casement windows were introduced to provide the illusion of daylight. The studio tower was entirely artificially ventilated; the air-conditioning plants were housed in the sub-basement. Thanks to Tudsbery, who found a way around the London County Council building regulations, Broadcasting House became the first building in London to have artificially ventilated toilets.

Fundamental changes during the design process included moving the Great Hall (Concert Hall – later to become the Radio Theatre) from the top floor to the lower ground floor, resulting in the redesign of the elevation above 80 feet. Tudsbery was aware that Reith

8

5 The site of BH at the top of Regent Street, in November 1928.

6+7 BH under construction during 1930, showing the steel frame and Portland Stone cladding. The advertisements on the construction hoardings depict familiar household products of the time and Joan Crawford in 'Our Blushing Brides', released in 1930.

8 BH shortly after completion in 1932. The studio tower can be seen protruding above the outer ring of offices.

did not like the original elevation but defended it, saying: 'The entrance as shown in the perspective only purported to be the entrance to a large corner bank, whilst the main entrance for the Corporation was to have been in the Portland Place facade.' In the end, of course, the banking hall was omitted and the entrance to the BBC stood in its place. The cost of BH reported in the press in 1930 was about £500,000 (£25m today).

The March 1931 issue of *Modern Wireless* described BH as 'built in the modern skyscraper fashion of steel frame work with concrete facing'. The outer office ring is steel frame construction, faced with Portland stone. The inner ring, 22 studios of varying sizes isolated from the offices by a corridor and constructed in a large studio tower, has solid brick walls (4 feet 6 inches at the base) without stanchions. The tower is expressed on the

9 BH with the circular portico of John Nash's All Souls church in the foreground. BH superseded the role of All Souls as the primary pivot between Upper Regent Street and Portland Place.

10+11 The Radio Theatre (Concert Hall) had more space for the orchestra than the audience. It had a partly flat, partly stepped floor. The strongly articulated piers and beams were meant to express the theatre's position in the centre of the building. The walls were decorated with a series of bas reliefs by Gilbert Bayes.

12 The Control Room was designed by Wells Coates and was a well-lit L-shaped room on the eighth floor, divided functionally into two halves. Eight control desks were provided for rehearsals and there were six control desks in the transmission section.

13 The semi-circular Council Chamber echoes the shape of the Entrance Hall below. It is lined with Tasmanian oak and used to be lit at night by reflected light from lamps concealed in wrought-oak urns, the pedestals of which provide accents of interest to the walls.

9

Portland Place elevation by the seven roundels, rather like portholes, rising above the office windows. Unfortunately, the symmetry of this west elevation is seldom appreciated due to its convexity. MacCormac Jamieson Prichard's heritage study of Broadcasting House notes that the 'streamlined facade was curiously mixed with an English sense of restraint. Myer's choice of a Georgian proportioned window unit with small panes demonstrated this conservatism ... The facades are interesting as they attempt to come to terms with the new developments in modernism and the expression of technology – but the elevation lacks the dynamic of an early modernist building, being symmetrical and formally composed.'

The ground-floor concert hall occupies almost the whole area within the walls of the studio tower, its splayed form providing good acoustics. A form of sea grass, 'eel grass', was dried, packaged in canvas quilts known as 'Cabot's Quilting' and packed in the cavity between the inner and outer walls of the studio tower as an early form of cavity-wall insulation.

Broadcasting House opened on 1 May 1932 and the BBC flag was flown for the first time on this day. The official opening of the new building as a broadcast centre was on 15 May. Sir John Reith recalled the move of 31 staff from Marconi House to Savoy Hill. Nine years later, the number had swelled to 'about seven hundred'. Despite the magnificence of the exterior there was some concern about the interior, although some of the country's best young designers had been commissioned. They included Raymond McGrath (decoration consultant), Wells Coates (news studio and production group) and Serge Chermayeff (eighth floor group of studios and a talks studio on the third floor). Assistant Controller Commander VH Goldsmith had managed to persuade the BBC to limit the number of traditional panelled interiors and to embrace a modern streamlined effect for the more technical rooms. Goldsmith had employed, in the opinion of *The Architectural Review* 'foresight and courage worthy of the best traditions of the BBC'. But despite the beauty and refinement of many of the spaces, still Reith wrote that he was 'not happy about the new Broadcasting House', and some of the staff were disappointed to leave Savoy Hill, commenting on the long, narrow offices and small studios of the new building. *The Review*, despite its lavish praise, also noted the 'labyrinth pokiness' of aspects of the interior. Neither the architect nor the client had predicted the prodigious rate with which the BBC would expand. Within weeks, the Corporation was bursting out of its new home. Soon only one office, on the third floor, was left

10

11

12

13

14

15

unoccupied and offices had to be subdivided to provide further accommodation.

Throughout the building process, Broadcasting House naturally received much interest in the press. The sculptures, by Eric Gill, attracted particular attention (as did the sculptor himself who neglected to wear underwear beneath his smock). The BBC suggested that he take the figure of Shakespeare's Ariel as the central theme; the invisible spirit of the air being a suitable personification of broadcasting. The two panels on the west elevation are of Ariel between Wisdom and Gaiety and Ariel hearing celestial music. Above the entrance stands Prospero, Ariel's master, sending him out into the world; and on the east elevation, situated above what was to be the entrance to the Children's Hour studio, is Ariel piping the children. Inside, a symbolic figure of The Sower, also by Gill, forms the centrepiece of the entrance hall. Directly opposite the entrance is a Latin inscription, the translation of which is: 'This temple of the arts and muses is dedicated to ALMIGHTY GOD by the first Governors of Broadcasting in the year 1931, Sir John Reith being Director-General. It is their prayer that good seed sown may bring forth a good harvest, that all things hostile to peace or purity may be banished from this house, and that the people, inclining their ear to whatsoever things are beautiful and honest and of good report, may tread the path of wisdom and uprightness.'

On completion, Professor CH Reilly of the architectural department of Liverpool University wrote in *The Listener*: 'The architect has taken the big curved front to Portland Place and modelled it in a series of flat vertical planes rising sheer from the pavement but balanced about a central axis. The windows in their long

14 Eric Gill's sculpture of 'Ariel piping the children' on the east elevation above what was to be the Children's Hour studio. Shakespeare's Ariel, as the invisible spirit of the air, was chosen as the personification of broadcasting.

15 The imposing sculpture 'Ariel in the arms of Prospero' showing Prospero sending Ariel out into the world stands above the entrance. Along with 'The Sower', in the entrance hall, it is the best-known of Gill's sculptures at BH.

16 Detail showing the clock above the entrance and the five-storey catslide roof of the east elevation. The Langham Street elevation is currently constrained by this last-minute addition to Val Myer's design. MJP will remove this roof and create larger floor plates for new operational accommodation.

16

17

17 The main entrance to BH, designed by Val Myer, has retained its 1930s design and semi-circular shape with very few modifications over the years.

18 Studio 4C, the foreign language studio in BH, photographed in 1938.

ranges emphasise admirably the curve of the front. Probably out of sympathy for the surrounding buildings, he has not turned them into long continuous sheets of glass in the modern way, but has given each the ordinary vertical shape.'

The Daily Express of 18 October 1930 proclaimed: 'New £500,000 home of wireless. Brain centre of modern civilisation. World's new voice. Will it become the most potent educational factor since Caxton first introduced his printing press into England?'

Broadcasting House was to be 'a factory for the production and reproduction of sound'. It fulfilled this practical brief, squeezing in 22 studios, one mile of corridors, 800 doors, 1250 stairs and 50 miles of electrical wiring. Despite the shortfall of the interior, it has become very much more than 'a factory'. The sleek building is now listed Grade II*. With its battleship prow facing the bustle of Regent Street and leaving in its wake the classical order of James Adam's Portland Place, it has withstood such indignities as direct bomb blasts in the Second World War and artless additions to the east flank. Even before the realisation of MJP's breathtaking addition, the original building stands proud; a comforting reminder to passers-by of the strength and stability of their nation's broadcaster.

Entering the doors of Broadcasting House for the first time, beneath Gill's Ariel in the arms of Prospero, visitors experience the thrill of stepping on hallowed ground. These are the doors through which the famous and infamous have swept. Along these corridors politicians and pop stars have hurried to take their seat in front of the microphone. This is where Prime Ministers have addressed the nation and philosophers, artists and scientists have delivered their Reith lectures.

The history of broadcasting seeps from the stone, but there is a tangible sense of a building clinging to the past, as if not really sure of its role in the present. It has long since failed to accommodate News and never became home to the World Service, although it was home to its predecessor, the Empire Service, before the war. The Portland stone is sensuous and architecturally sensitive to the surrounding buildings, but it doesn't offer the transparency so needed to fulfil the aims of the BBC's new property strategy. It is for this reason that a competition was set up to find an architect who could deliver a 21st-century vision for the headquarters of the BBC, bringing it a new vitality and openness while respecting the grandeur and dignity of the 1932 building.

18

1 Foster Associates won the competition to put forward proposals for a new radio headquarters on the site of the Langham Hotel opposite BH. This concept sketch, dated 1982, shows the view of All Souls from a studio.

THE LEARNING CURVE

The BBC's property portfolio includes several projects that, despite enormous financial, intellectual and emotional investment, never saw the light of day. The most significant of these is the scheme developed by Norman Foster in the 1980s for Langham Place. The history of this commission and its abandonment needs to be understood before considering MacCormac Jamieson Prichard's current scheme for Broadcasting House.

In the early 1980s, Foster was already well on the way to attaining the international reputation that he now enjoys, with work such as Willis Faber and Dumas in Ipswich, the Sainsbury Centre for Visual Arts in Norwich and the Hongkong and Shanghai Bank, Hong Kong, to his name. In 1982 Foster Associates, today known as Foster and Partners, was invited by the BBC to participate in an international limited competition to put forward proposals for developing first a brief, then a design, for a new radio headquarters on the site of the Langham Hotel opposite Broadcasting House. The Langham was owned and occupied by the BBC at the time. Foster won the competition from a shortlist that included Terry Farrell and Partners and Arup Associates, and had initially extended to Richard Rogers, Kevin Roche and IM Pei. It was to become what senior partner and project architect Spencer de Grey calls 'one of the three great unbuilt projects of our practice – on a par with Hammersmith [a transport interchange, office complex and public space project for London Transport, 1977] and the athletics stadium in Frankfurt [1981]'.

The scheme was huge, complex and, for the time, unusually transparent. In the 1980s, very few top-flight architects were being commissioned by the BBC and there was little architectural vision within the Corporation. Foster's scheme represented a first on many levels. His practice worked on the project for five years, almost to the point of applying for planning permission. Although it was never built, it is still referred to regularly by senior partners today.

As de Grey says: 'After Willis Faber [Ipswich, 1971-75], Hammersmith and the Hong Kong bank, Langham was our next major exploration of a key city site – the whole concept of public space and private realm and how you link the two. We took it extraordinarily seriously. We explored a number of ideas that have taken root in later work. You could say that the public space at Langham was a precursor for the Great Court at the British Museum. For us it was a seminal work, and it's no accident that it was displayed alongside the Hong Kong bank at the Foster, Rogers,

1

2 Perspective of Fosters' Langham scheme showing a typical studio, left, with control cubicle, right, both on spring mounts and flanked by circulation and service zones.

3 Long section showing the new building in the context of BH and All Souls.

2

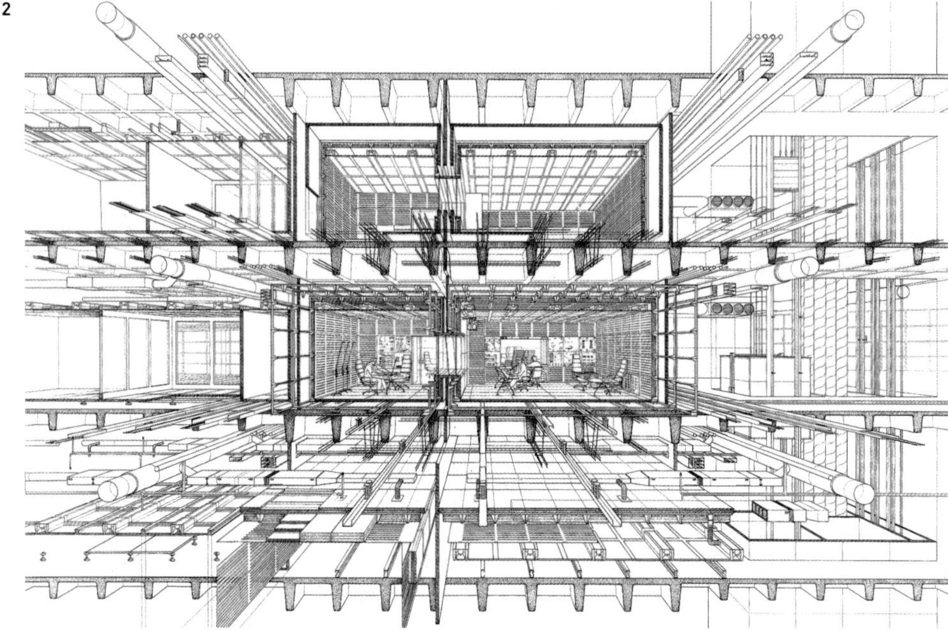

Stirling show at the Royal Academy [1986]. It's a project we were very proud of and we were very sad it didn't go ahead.' Had the BBC been able or willing to embrace a partnership with the private sector, things might have been different.

The Architectural Review of May 1987 wept over the loss of 'one of the most elegant and assured new buildings that Londoners have had within their grasp for some time'. The magazine headline 'Foster at the BBC – A New Glasnost' suggested the scale of the missed opportunity – a chance to usher in a new era of openness and forthrightness for the BBC. As the literal translation of the Russian word 'glasnost' is 'speaking aloud' it was all the more appropriate for a broadcaster.

In fact, the competition brief had called for an analysis of the BBC's accommodation, rather than a building, in the first instance. The BBC was keen to see the architect's approach to designing a building for it. The report put together by the Foster team charted new territory in the practice's approach to competition submissions. At the interview the architects demonstrated a number of massing possibilities and approaches, and subsequently developed the brief with the client. De Grey adds: 'That was done by us and the office planning group we'd worked with on the bank, the Quickborner team from Hamburg, who were responsible for developing Burolandschaft in America in the late 1960s and 1970s.'

The brief included building up records of personnel, who was in which department and where they were located. At the time, there were approximately 6000 employees occupying about 96,000 square metres in the W1 area, therefore excluding Television Centre and Bush House.

'We tried to work out how they related to other departments, which was revealing. We began to identify a range of different spaces and space standards for different activities, and built up the brief from first principles', says de Grey.

A studio mock-up was built in the basement of the Langham building, and all-day workshops helped to create consensus among the legendary warring tribes. Dick Francis, Managing Director, Radio, was the architect's day-to-day client and key to the success of this co-operation.

Despite the tribal nature of the organisation, Foster saw the BBC as dynamic, communicative and exciting. *The Architectural Review* evocatively describes the practice 'clinging to an image of transparency, of revelation – of an apparently solid block whose one chamfered corner was carved

3

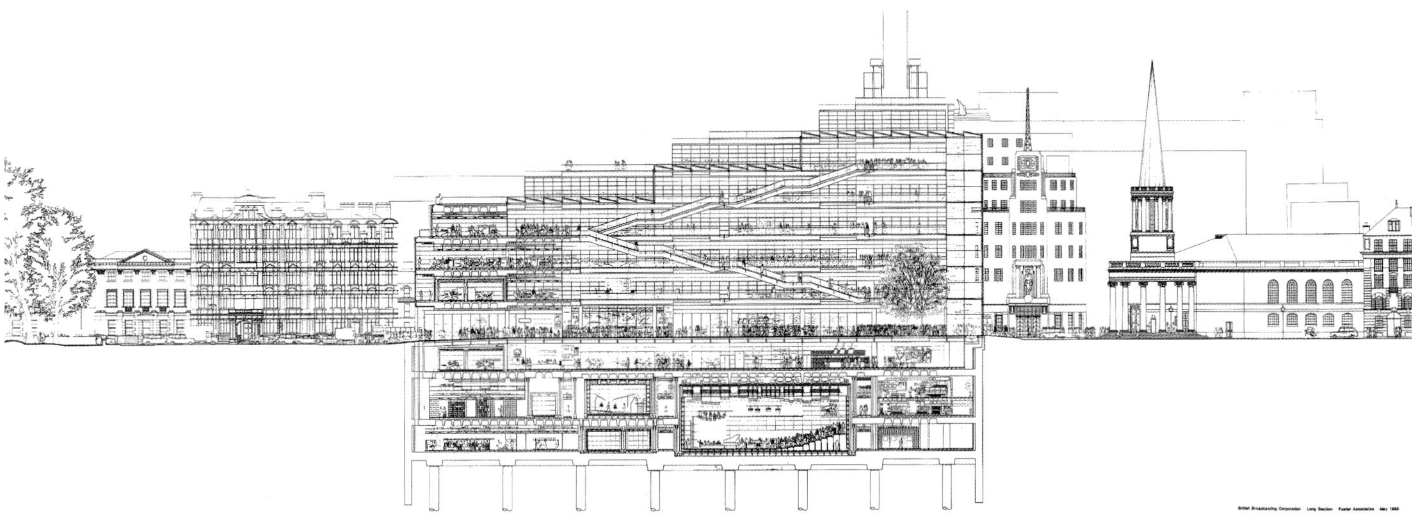

away by a huge glazed gash, or atrium, to reveal, like complex microchip circuitry, the mass of blips and bleeps and humans and tiny flashing lights that constitutes the inner sacred workings of the BBC'.

The Langham Hotel, which was to be demolished in the Foster scheme, stands on the pivotal site between the bustling retail of Regent Street and Oxford Circus to the south, and the professional and residential precinct of Portland Place to the north. The first building on this site, Foley House, was built by Lord Foley and designed by James Wyatt in 1786. The site was leased from the Duke of Portland on the condition that the views of fields and heathland to the north should remain uninterrupted. Queen Anne's Square was to stand in front of it, but this was superseded by the Adam brothers' plan for Portland Place, which at 100 feet was the same width as Foley House. It was, in the 18th century, possibly the grandest street in London.

The 19th century brought further changes, with the elevation in 1811 of the Prince of Wales to the Regency and the creation of the sequence of parks and streets from St James's Park to Regent's Park. At the request of the Prince Regent, John Nash planned a triumphal route from his royal residence, Carlton House, to the proposed Regent's Park, with Park Crescent serving as the gateway. Foley House presented an obstacle to his plans, but this was soon overcome when it was discovered that Lord Foley was in financial straits. His house was bought and demolished. Langham House was built and aligned to the west side of Portland Place. But pressure from powerful residents in Cavendish Square, behind Langham House, put a stop to Nash's plans to continue the new route directly south, and the street was pushed 300 feet to the east, resulting in the S-curve of Langham Place, acknowledged and enhanced by the circular portico of Nash's All Souls Church.

Pevsner described the Langham Hotel, which replaced Langham House in 1864 as 'a High Victorian monster'. It was not as sensitive to the S-bend and its corner turret, which would at least have been a gesture to the peculiar nature of the site, was blown off by a bomb, presumably intended for Broadcasting House.

In terms of planning, a cluster of four vertical elements highlighted in the Foster scheme, including the spire of All Souls and the prow of Broadcasting House, gave strength to the knuckle joint where Regent Street ends and Portland Place begins. The diagonal orientation of the scheme resulted from the diagonal axis across Cavendish Square,

4

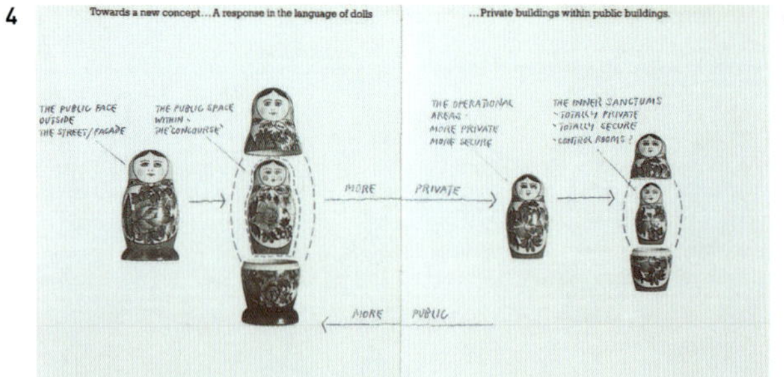

5

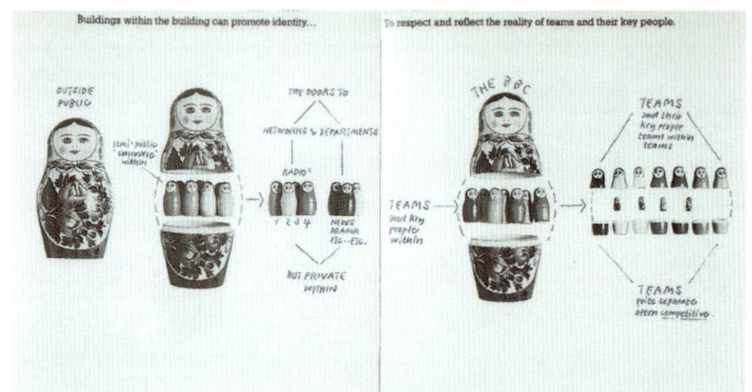

6

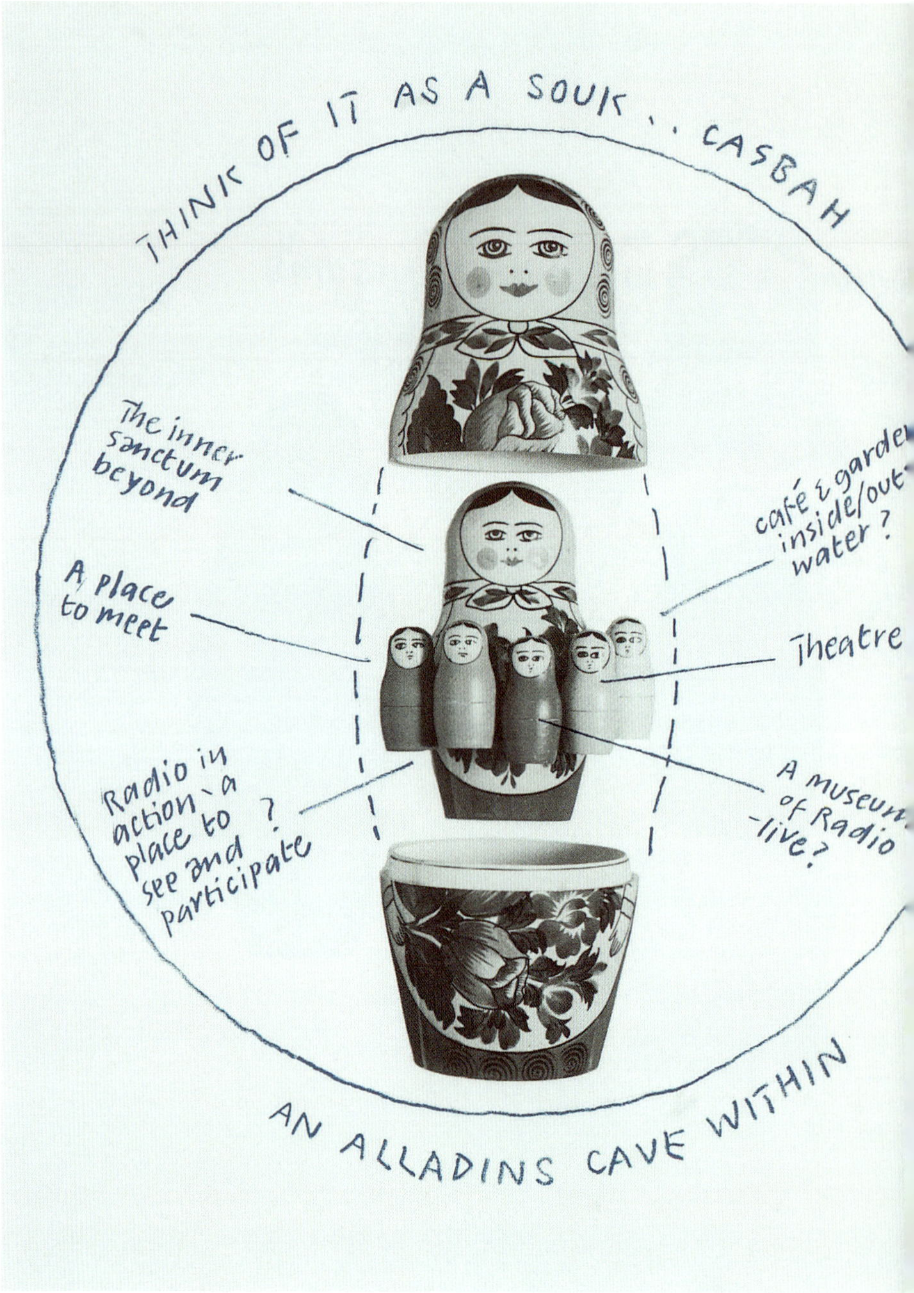

4 Norman Foster produced a series of sketches with Russian dolls to illustrate the life he envisaged within Langham Place. This first one he entitled 'Towards a new concept...A response in the language of dolls ...Private buildings within public buildings.'

5 'Buildings within the building can promote identity. To respect and reflect the reality of teams and their key people.'

6 'The souk...Old and new models.' The emphasis on the new is openness and visibility.

CLOSED NOW . . . BUT COULD BE OPENED UP . . . TO BECOME A SHOWCASE
FOR THE GLITTERING JEWEL
OF RADIO WITHIN

PAST ⟶ FUTURE ?

the tower of All Souls to the British Telecom Tower half a mile away, which was at that time the main distribution point for the BBC's programme signals. It is on this axis that the transparent atrium would have sat, providing light and giving views from Cavendish Square to All Souls, with a public mall running beneath.

Perhaps surprisingly, de Grey's sadness at losing this prestigious commission does not appear to be tinged with bitterness. He believes the practice evolved significantly as a result of the work on Langham Place. 'Our solution for Langham was an antidote to the introverted. You could say the same of the Great Court, which opens up the British Museum, and also Nîmes [médiathèque] and the Reichstag. The importance of public space runs through much of our work and had its origins in the Hong Kong bank, where the banking hall has a public space that flows beneath. At Langham it was taken several steps further.'

He is also confident that the BBC took note of much of the Foster research, even if subconsciously. This is obvious when he talks of what the Langham building could have achieved. His words might have been uttered by Alan Yentob, Jenny Abramsky, Director, Radio and Music or John Smith today.

'The idea of housing radio in one building was a new concept for the BBC and it would have been great – giving a face to something otherwise intangible. I feel it was a lost opportunity for transforming radio. The public spaces could have been used for interviewing, among other things, ending the barrier between radio and the public it served. With its location at the end of the world's longest shopping street you'd have had vox pop outside your door. It would have added

7 Aerial view of the model of Langham Place looking down on the giant mall.

8 Street-level view, with All Souls in the foreground.

9 The importance of large, open public spaces in the work of Foster Associates had its origins in the Hongkong and Shanghai Bank. This was taken further in Langham Place, and the project, although never built, has played a crucial role in the development of the practice.

9

10 Sketch by Norman Foster showing the site with the profile of the existing Langham Hotel. Although the building successfully negotiates the turn in the street, he bemoans the lack of a public space.

11 A sketch by Norman Foster concentrating on the inviting nature of All Souls in contrast to the hotel.

10

another dimension. It would have been richer, more dynamic.'

So why was it pushed to one side? 'As an architect, you never totally know the reason why a project is cancelled. At a simple level, I think it was a complete change of direction of the BBC's property strategy, and a change of personnel.' George Howard, Chairman of the BBC and client and patron of Foster Associates, retired in 1985. He was replaced by Stuart Young, the former head of supermarket chain Tesco, who had little or no interest in architecture. Young turned his gaze to a greyhound track next to Television Centre in White City on which he would build a less complex and far cheaper building. Alan James, an in-house architect at the BBC, says Young 'had knowledge of acquiring and developing suburban plots of land in an efficient, quick and economic way but without any design

11

'THERE IS NO 'LANGHAM PLACE' - NASH HAD A GARDEN HERE.
COMPARE THE AGRESSION OF THIS CORNER WITH THE 'INVITATION' OF ALL SOULS!
NOTE HOW THE LEVEL CHANGE LIFTS YOU ABOVE THE TRAFFIC 'VISUALLY BUT ALSO SMELLS - A BETTER PROSPECT THAN PAVEMENT LEVEL.
NF
NOTE HOW THE PERISTYLE IS INVITING - A PUBLIC SPACE - A SYMPATHETIC GESTURE - PEOPLE SIT ON THE STEPS EVEN IN THE COLDEST WEATHER!

12

13

input. He was a proponent of what was just emerging as design build.' James also believes that cost was an insurmountable issue on the Langham project. It was going to cost much more than originally intended and there was not enough in the original budget. But more significantly: 'The BBC began to lose heart and Dick Francis, the head of Radio, was the only champion left after George Howard resigned.'

Part of the equity in the White City bid was the sale of the Langham island site. The old hotel – the first of the large Victorian hotels to be built away from a railway terminus – was being used by the BBC for radio training, the BBC club and bedrooms for presenters, and one of the issues of the Foster scheme was justifying the demolition of a listed building. It was decided that White City would become the new BBC headquarters. And so was born 'the tin shed', built by Balfour Beatty with architect Scott Brownrigg Turner. The building has been problematic, to say the least, since the beginning. Although most of the corporate staff moved to White City, the Director-General and Chairman, by then John Birt and Christopher Bland, preferred to stay in Broadcasting House.

As Radio's Head of Engineering and later as Controller, Property, George Crowe was involved with the Langham project from the beginning. Now retired, he says: 'Not only did we lose a fine building and a huge opportunity for technical innovation, we also lost the opportunity to open up the BBC and transform it from a "corridor culture". Only now is the organisation beginning to move in that way.'

David Chipperfield worked for Foster Associates on the project. Now a successful and internationally renowned architect in his own right, he sees what happened at Langham Place as a warning for Pacific Quay, the BBC Scotland project he is designing in Glasgow. 'It was a financial decision in a way. White City was the result. The vision had been lost [by the client]. As soon as you lose your vision there's nothing that guides it any more.

'Langham was a classic case of an institution having a crisis about itself. That's always the problem when an organisation has to commission a new building [without a clear strategy]. It starts off as an accommodation problem ... and turns into a self-analysis, psychotherapy session with enormous consequences if those are not done well.

'Essentially the BBC hasn't changed much since then, but there are few higher up the tree, like Alan [Yentob] and John [Smith] and Greg Dyke who are convinced now that it's worth standing up to the accountant mentality. What you had in Langham Place was George Howard and Dick Francis who had a really vivid

14

15

and romantic vision in the Reithian tradition. We shouldn't forget that the BBC has built one of the great 20th-century buildings in London. They didn't want to give up that tradition. That hit head-on with the Thatcher ethos and Stuart Young, who did a pragmatic series of calculations. Some things are more important than that and have a value themselves. I think the mood has changed. There's a realisation that having a good building and good environment is fundamental to your organisation.'

12+13 Phase 1 of White City by Scott Brownrigg Turner was to be followed by Phase 2, a headquarters for News & Current Affairs (shown here, designed by RHWL) and Phase 3, for Radio. This would have brought the BBC together at Wood Lane, with Television just down the road at TVC. RHWL was commissioned in 1989 and the project progressed as far as the selection of a contractor. It was pulled by the Director-General Michael Checkland. He was coming to the end of his first 5 year tenure and instead of being reappointed was succeeded by his deputy, John Birt.

14 The failure to build Phases 2 and 3 of White City resulted in a bid to spend money on BH to tidy up the radio accommodation. A proposal was made for what was to become known as BHX (designed in-house and subsequently by Fletcher Priest). At the same time there was a proposal to rebuild the orchestral studio at Maida Vale, also by RHWL (shown here). The projects were to cost around £10m each, and Checkland gave Radio the choice of one or other of the two proposals. BHX went ahead and the Maida Vale studio was pulled. RHWL finally won and completed a BBC contract for a drama studio, Maida Vale 6, in 1992.

15 In the late 1990s there was also a move to look at ways of accommodating News and the World Service together in one building. Several sites were considered, but Bush House was deemed the best. Foster and Partners produced a design concept for Bush House in 1998 but, although popular with the BBC, the development deal proved too difficult to broker with the Japanese owners of the blocks leased to the BBC.

16

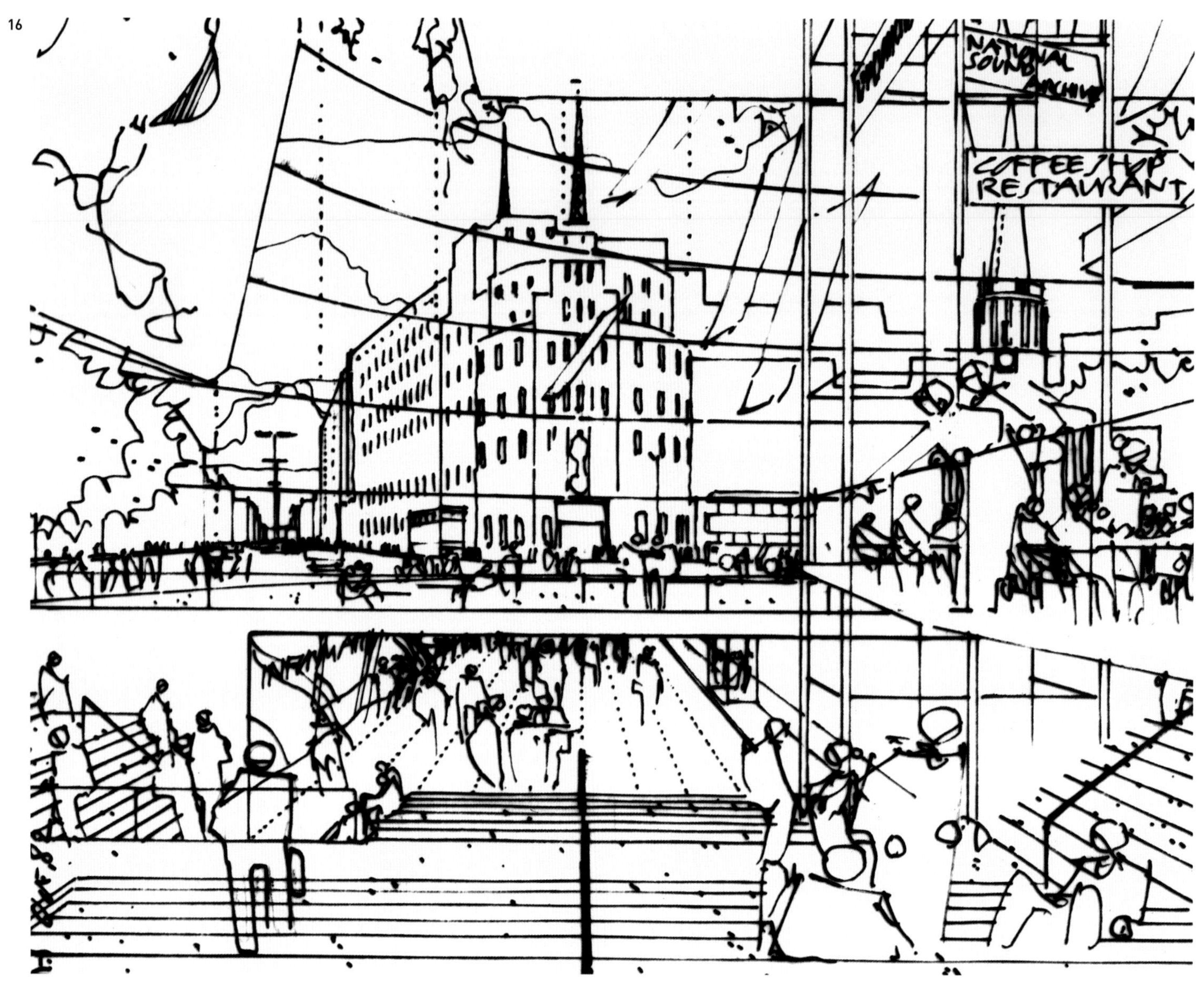

16 Concept sketch of Langham scheme by Foster Associates.

4

THE NEW BROADCASTING HOUSE

1 Competition sketch. Section showing a new Langham Place, to be used by the public as well as the BBC, the huge atrium and the newsroom.

THE NEW BROADCASTING HOUSE

Broadcasting House is already one of London's best-loved buildings, listed Grade II in 1981 and upgraded to Grade II* in 1995. It harbours 70 years of history within its stone walls and reflects the strength of the BBC as a national institution. MacCormac Jamieson Prichard's scheme for its redesign and extension shows every sign of preserving the cultural, political and architectural history embedded in the building while propelling the new headquarters into the spotlight as the most significant new cultural building in the capital. The MJP project is part of the BBC's three-site strategy for London. BH will be the headquarters and the home of all news and radio; Television Centre will be returned to its original purpose as a television production factory, and White City will become a mixed media village (see Chapter 6, pages 88-89).

Although BH has been the official headquarters of the BBC since 1932, MJP's project will put it back at the centre of the UK's broadcasting universe. With accommodation for all radio stations, all television and radio news and the entire World Service operation, BH will be the nerve centre of the Corporation. It will house the largest newsroom in the world, as well as an impressive 140 studios and 20 miles of cabling. The building's population will swell to some 3500 staff and visitors. The complexity of the scheme has required the practice to produce more than 1500 drawings (up to the end of summer 2002), and to expand its studio to house the additional architects taken on to work solely on the BBC project.

Of course, the modernist building of 1932 – which was in many ways quite radical when seen in the context of the Regency buildings and the Adam-designed streets around it – has evolved significantly, for better or worse, over the intervening years. Dramatic changes in broadcasting needs and production techniques, as well as damage sustained during the Second World War, have left indelible marks on the Val Myer original. Broadcasting House suffered bomb damage on three separate occasions. Although the exterior was restored successfully, the pioneering and diverse designs for the interiors by Val Myer, Raymond McGrath, Wells Coates and Serge Chermayeff were all lost within a decade of completion, with the single exception of the Concert Hall (now the Radio Theatre). Gone too are all the bespoke fittings and furniture, and the long, thin Control Room (with its original technical equipment) by Wells Coates.

The opportunity to redesign the studios was turned to the BBC's advantage, as they were rearranged to meet the changing needs of

1

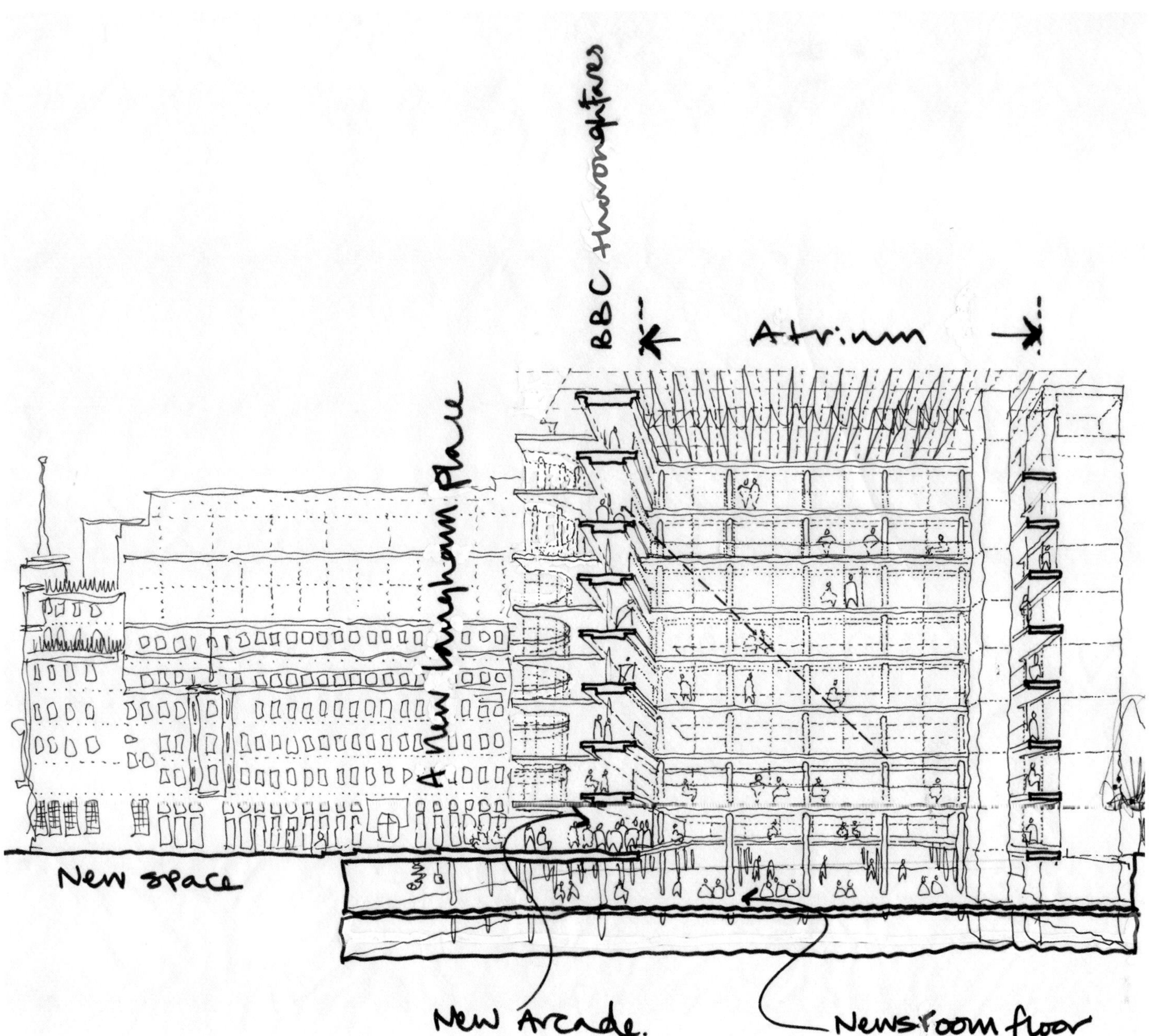

BBC thoroughfares
Atrium
A New Langham Place
New space
New Arcade.
Newsroom floor

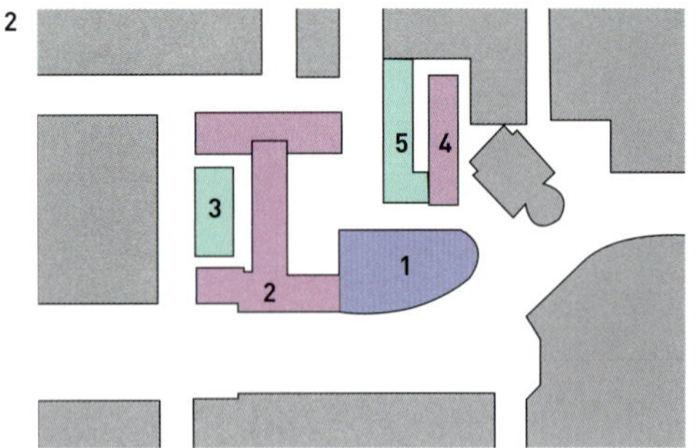

2 Diagrammatic site plan of existing BH site.
Key:
1 BH
2 BHX
3 BHXX
4 Egton House
5 16 Langham Street

broadcasting operations. Pairs of studios and cubicles replaced the original layouts leading to a radical reconfiguration of the division walls within the studio tower. In some areas whole damaged floor slabs were left unreplaced in order to create larger volumes, as on the seventh floor. Since then, there have been successive phases of reorganisation and refurbishment within the studio tower, and there are some studios outside the tower. Many studios moved to the basement of the Broadcasting House extension, known as the BHX building and completed in 1959.

MJP's extensive heritage study of Broadcasting House lists the most significant changes in the recent past as the insertion of a mezzanine at eighth-floor level to provide additional office space; the demolition and extensions to the north party wall in 1981; the refitting of the Radio Theatre in 1994; the escalator connection to BHX in 1994; the completion of the BBC shop in 1997; the refurbishment of the main entrance hall (most recently in 1998); the remodelling of offices at third floor to open plan in 2000 by DEGW; and the relocation of roof-top services and associated remodelling. Reading this list today and then walking the corridors of Broadcasting House, one gets an impression of disarray; a patch-up job that has finally given way at the seams. Many of the interventions, including the open-plan offices on the third floor designed by DEGW, have been chinks of light in the otherwise grey armour of the workspaces. They are an indication that the BBC has been aware for some time that it needed to do something about Broadcasting House, and indeed its whole property portfolio.

In 1997, the 2020 Property Vision Project was launched and, in October that year, the BBC invited Nick Morgan and Stephen Bradley of DEGW to offer advice on how to go about changing the workspaces across all departments of the BBC. 'We wanted views about current thinking on the workplace, about trends and outside influences. I'd heard about what DEGW had done for Andersens in Chicago, and was keen to get them involved,' says John Dee, now Head of Interior Design.

During the winter of 1997 and into the first few months of 1998, DEGW was commissioned to do eight pilot studies, resulting in the design of new workspaces for Will Wyatt, head of BBC Broadcast. Director-General John Birt liked what he saw and commissioned DEGW to design a new 'corporate' floor within Broadcasting House. DEGW's task, under Morgan, was to map the diversity of the BBC and to make sense of the technical and artistic needs of individual teams while making the

4

5

3 Workspace of Pat Loughrey, Director, Nations and Regions. The open-plan office, designed by DEGW, was one of a series of offices in the Corporate Centre on the third floor of BHX.

4 A Business Lounge was incorporated by DEGW into the Corporate Centre. It provided BBC personnel from outside BH with a place to work when they visited central London.

5 Small meeting rooms and breakout spaces were designed alongside open-plan offices.

6

7

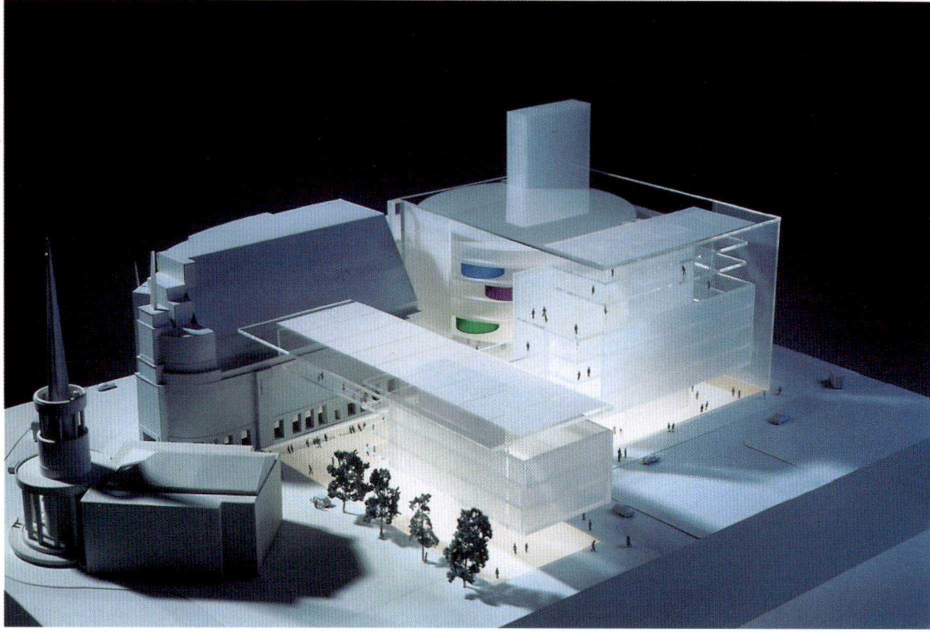

working areas less cellular and more accessible. The pilot study spaces, although pretty conservative, revolutionised offices within Broadcasting House by getting rid of the long dark corridors and closed doors and providing light, open spaces with senior personnel sitting in the middle of them. The Corporate Centre on the third floor of BHX included a Business Lounge where BBC personnel from outside central London could work when visiting Broadcasting House. As this book goes to press, the DEGW pilot schemes are being dismantled to make way for the new Broadcasting House. The pilots showed senior executives that open plan collaborative working could work. What the pilots lacked was strength of identity for the individual teams. This is vital in a tribal organisation like the BBC and is being addressed in the work DEGW is doing for the new White City campus.

Between the work by DEGW and the competition for the new Broadcasting House, Llewelyn-Davies was appointed to undertake an architectural and planning study of BH and its adjacent buildings. The work, led by Steve Featherstone, was completed in 1999 and presented to the BBC governors in early 2000. It proved a critical turning-point for the project and informed the design brief for the subsequent competition.

The competition was co-ordinated by Programme Manager Joanna Streeten, who trained as a chartered engineer and is a long-standing BBC broadcasting engineer. BBC Project Director Chris Evans describes her role as 'perhaps equivalent to that of Tudsbery alongside Val Myer'. External advisers to the BBC included Ricky Burdett and Sir Stuart Lipton. Lipton was impressed by the BBC's attitude towards the selection process.

6 Competition scheme by Alsop & Störmer Architects.

7 Competition scheme by Stanton Williams.

8 Competition scheme by Eric Parry.

9 Competition scheme by Fletcher Priest Architects.

8

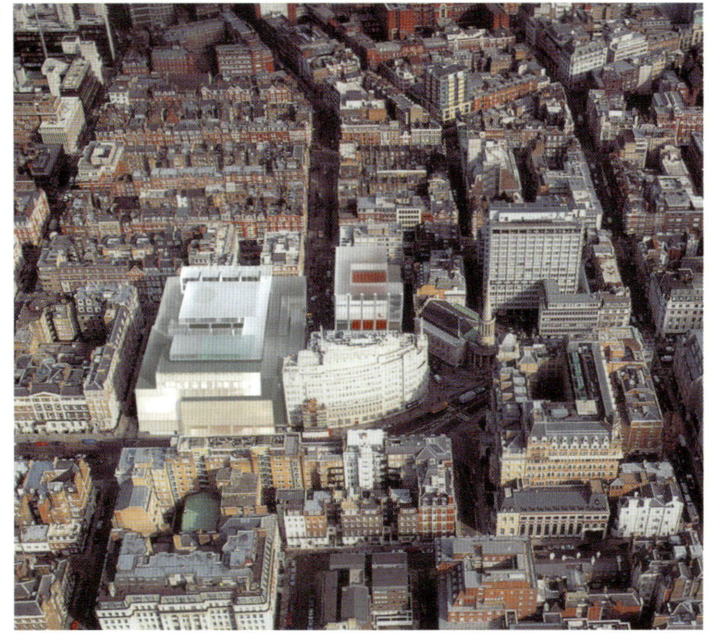

9

'Immediately we were treated as insiders and could demonstrate that best value was not necessarily the lowest cost. The most unusual part of the process was the full involvement of the chairman and most of the directors throughout. There was tangible excitement and enthusiasm and an understanding of the value of the art to the value of business.' Burdett helped to write the competition brief and ensure that an impressive calibre of architects was invited to pitch for the job. The shortlist included Alsop & Störmer, Eric Parry Architects, Fletcher Priest and Stanton Williams alongside eventual winner MacCormac Jamieson Prichard.

MJP's previous buildings include the Wellcome Wing of the Science Museum, the University of Lancaster's Ruskin Library, the training college for Cable & Wireless in Coventry and Southwark Jubilee Line Tube station. 'It was a curious competition', recalls Richard MacCormac, referring to the regular visits that BBC representatives made to MJP's office throughout the process. It was a sensible tactic and meant that the client could see each team's method of working and learn something about the personalities. 'It made us sharpen up our act,' admits MacCormac, who produced a more discursive, written presentation than his competitors. His team resisted the temptation to provide a more highly resolved solution, fearing that in trying to solve the whole problem it would lose sight of what the client really wanted. Instead, the practice focused on the way in which a new building might capture Greg Dyke's vision of 'One BBC'. 'We established a very simple circulation diagram right from the beginning, which showed what it might be like and where things could happen.'

MacCormac believes that MJP's success with the BBC competition depended on three things: first, the architect's appreciation and understanding of the BBC's culture and way of working; second, its impressive track record in seeing difficult projects through the planning application process and finally its ability to organise rational workspace. Planning consent for Broadcasting House was always going to be tough, given that the original building is listed Grade II* and stands in the middle of a conservation area under the jurisdiction of Westminster City Council. Fortunately, the architect and the BBC's Project Director Chris Evans and Andrew Fullerton (the BBC's Head of Environmental Planning) cleared this potential hurdle on 27 June 2002, but it was a long and arduous process. At every stage the team has had the full support of John Smith, the project's enthusiastic and committed sponsor.

10

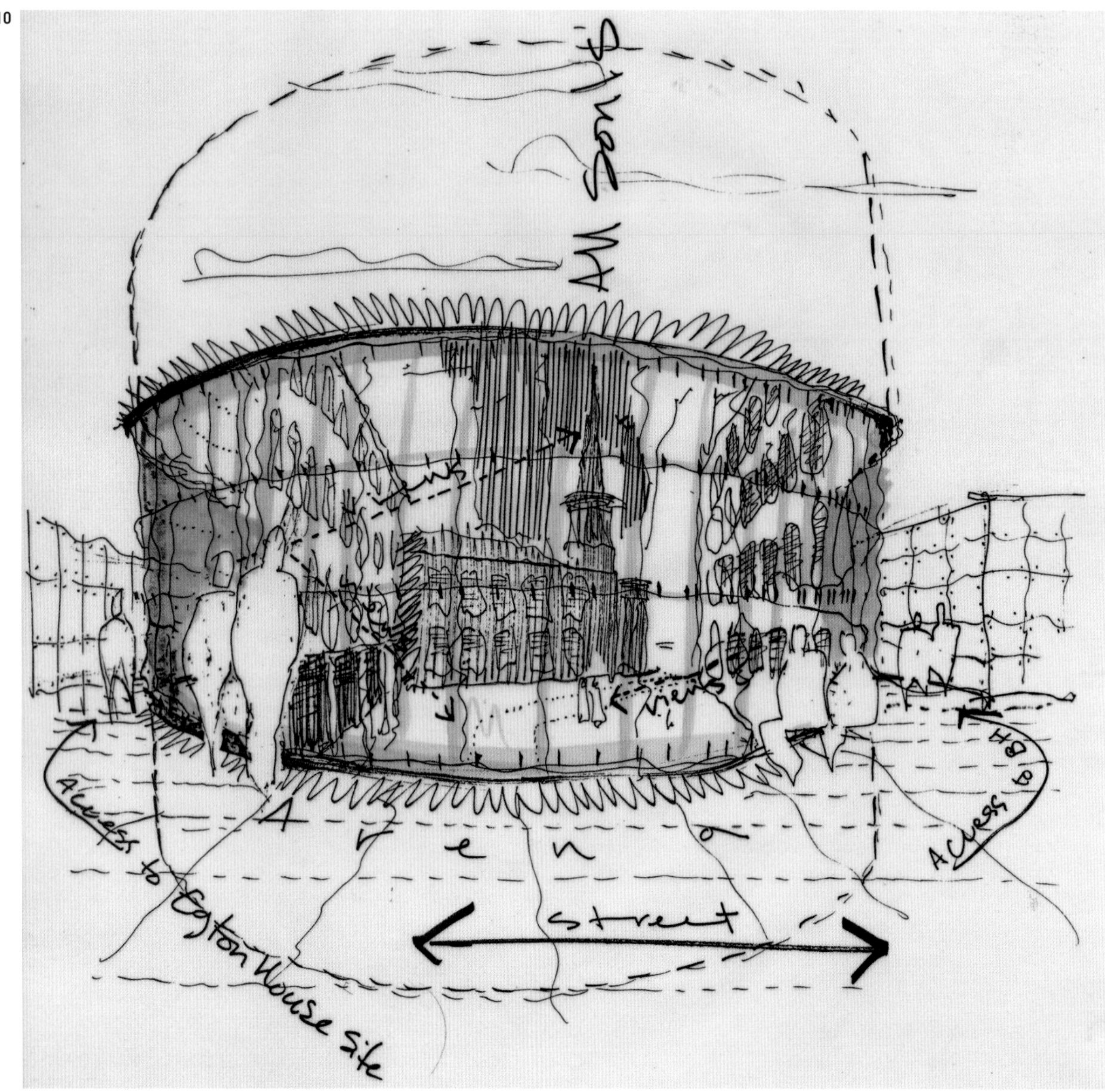

10 MJP competition sketch showing view from internal street looking out onto the public arena.

11

11 MJP competition sketch showing the proximity to All Souls church and the way in which the architecture will invite the public into the BBC.

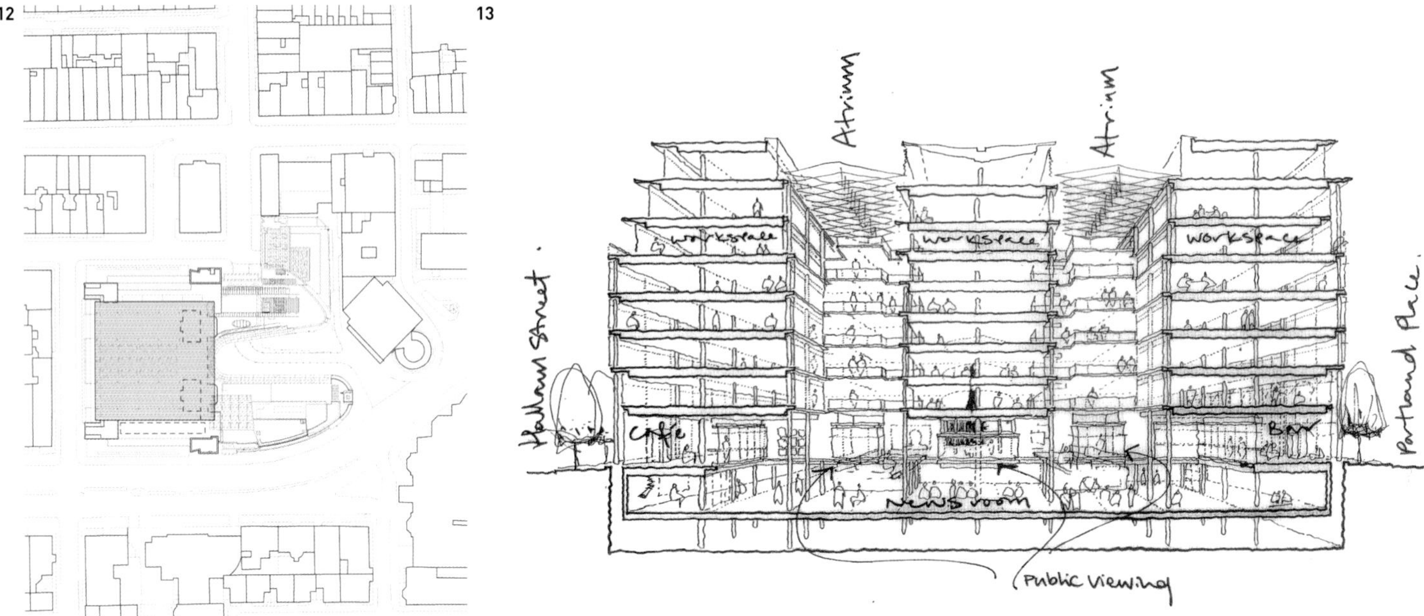

Alan Yentob describes MacCormac's pitch as 'brilliant. It's a respectful extension rather than a radical transformation.' This comment, intended as a compliment, sounds as though Yentob thinks the scheme rather conservative. Apparently not. At public meetings and in private conversation, he is quite obviously wowed by the beauty and drama of the project. 'Richard's scheme is very platonic. It's about one BBC sharing space while giving people their own territories. Intelligent pragmatism is what got him the building – and winning over the diverse clients. He understood our values and the BBC ended up with a building that is more than the sum of its parts.'

MJP's project architect on Broadcasting House, Mike Evans, was responsible for researching the heritage study on the building and the surrounding area with fellow director Mark Hines. In answer to criticisms from conservation groups that the new Broadcasting House would be too overbearing for the site, MJP was able to offer evidence that, historically, most of the great institutions in London were also discordant in scale. In Sir John Summerson's *Georgian London*, the author identified a period from the 1770s to the 1830s during which the architectural image of London moved from one of a mass of housing elevations (with the exception of St Paul's and Wren's churches in the City) to 'an image of rich interest' due to the investment in prominent public and private buildings. Their outsize scale signified their importance. In order to demonstrate the place of BH in this evolutionary process, Evans and Hines commissioned a photographer to take pictures of some of these great monumental buildings, such as the Albert Hall, the Royal Institution and the Royal Opera House. MacCormac

12 Site plan of the MacCormac Jamieson Prichard scheme.

13 MJP competition sketch. Section showing two full height atria opening up the interior from the giant newsroom at lower ground floor level.

14 MJP competition sketch showing departmental front doors opening onto the internal street.

14

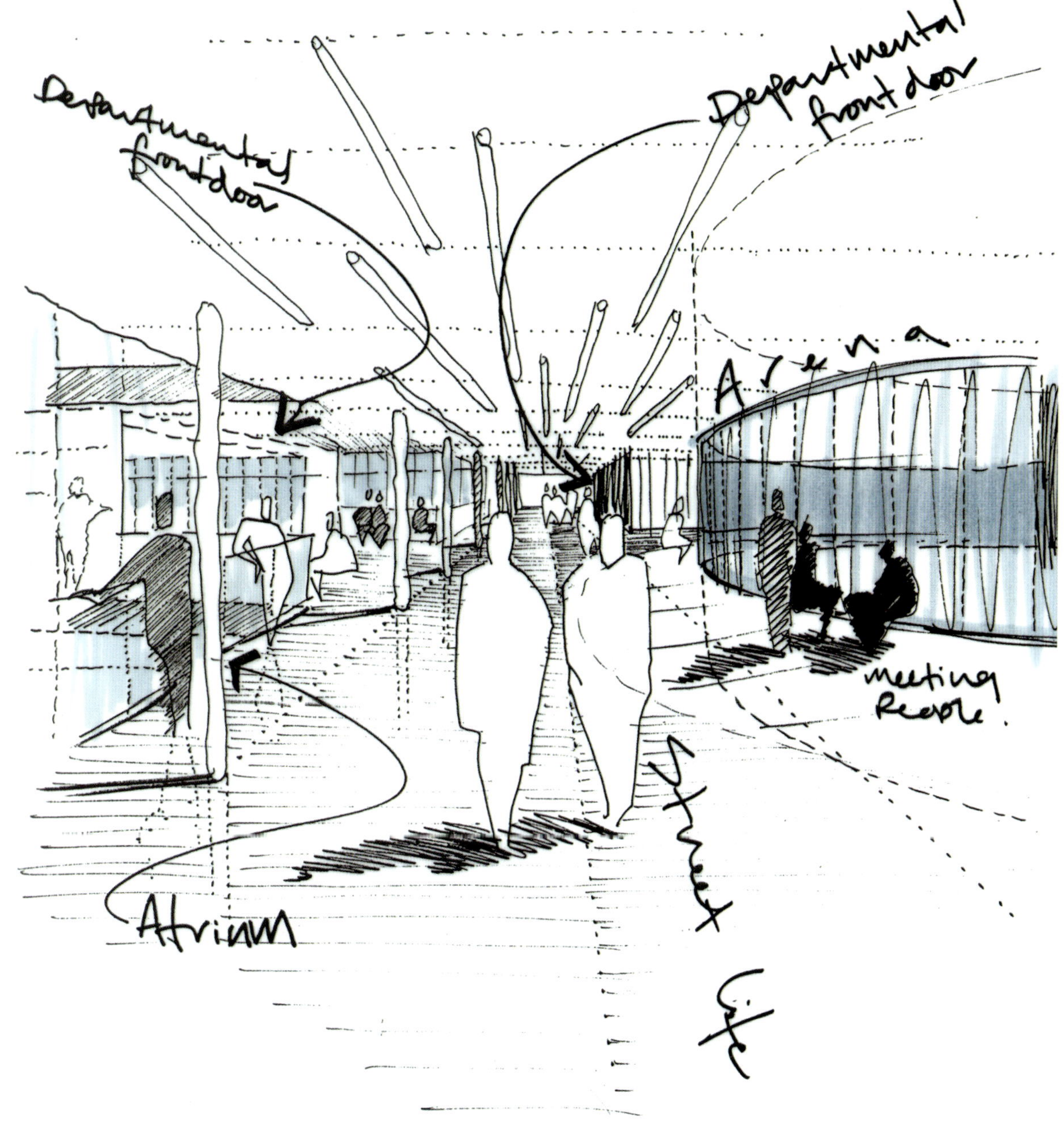

Departmental front door
Departmental front door
Arena
meeting People
Street Life
Atrium

15

explains how the images had the desired effect on the London Advisory Committee of English Heritage: 'I said, here's the north-east corner of the Royal Opera House adjacent to an 1820 townhouse half its height. Here is the British Museum and here is a bit of Bloomsbury which it dominates, and everyone suddenly understood. In our case, here you have a national institution and alongside it the Georgian scale of Nash and Adam. This is the way it always was, until conservation officers started to believe that everything had to be the same scale.'

For the public, the focus of MJP's new development will be the public space in Langham Street, the area scooped out between the prow of the original BH and its new counterpart on the Egton House site. Plans are afoot to use this outdoor arena for public events, such as theatre and dance, as well as debates and concerts. There are ambitious ideas for a public art programme at BH, much of which will focus on this arena and will attract the public and give them another reason to walk up from Oxford Circus. These ideas are expanded upon in Chapter 9. The hope is that Broadcasting House will become a central venue for the annual Regent Street Festival, which takes place in September, and it could also become the focus for the street's famous Christmas lights. From a practical point of view this public space will provide a logical culmination to the retail frenzy of Regent Street, with shops and restaurants opening onto the space. The Radio Theatre Café and BBC shop, which will occupy its two long elevations, may also be accessed from here. In recognition of the British climate, a glass canopy has been designed for the perimeter despite the sheltered, southern aspect.

15 Sketch showing the use of the public space in the arena. Cafés and shops will spill out into the open air. There are plans for other public events, including concerts and shows.

16 Axonometric projection giving a view into the Radio Theatre and the arena set up as an outdoor theatre.

16

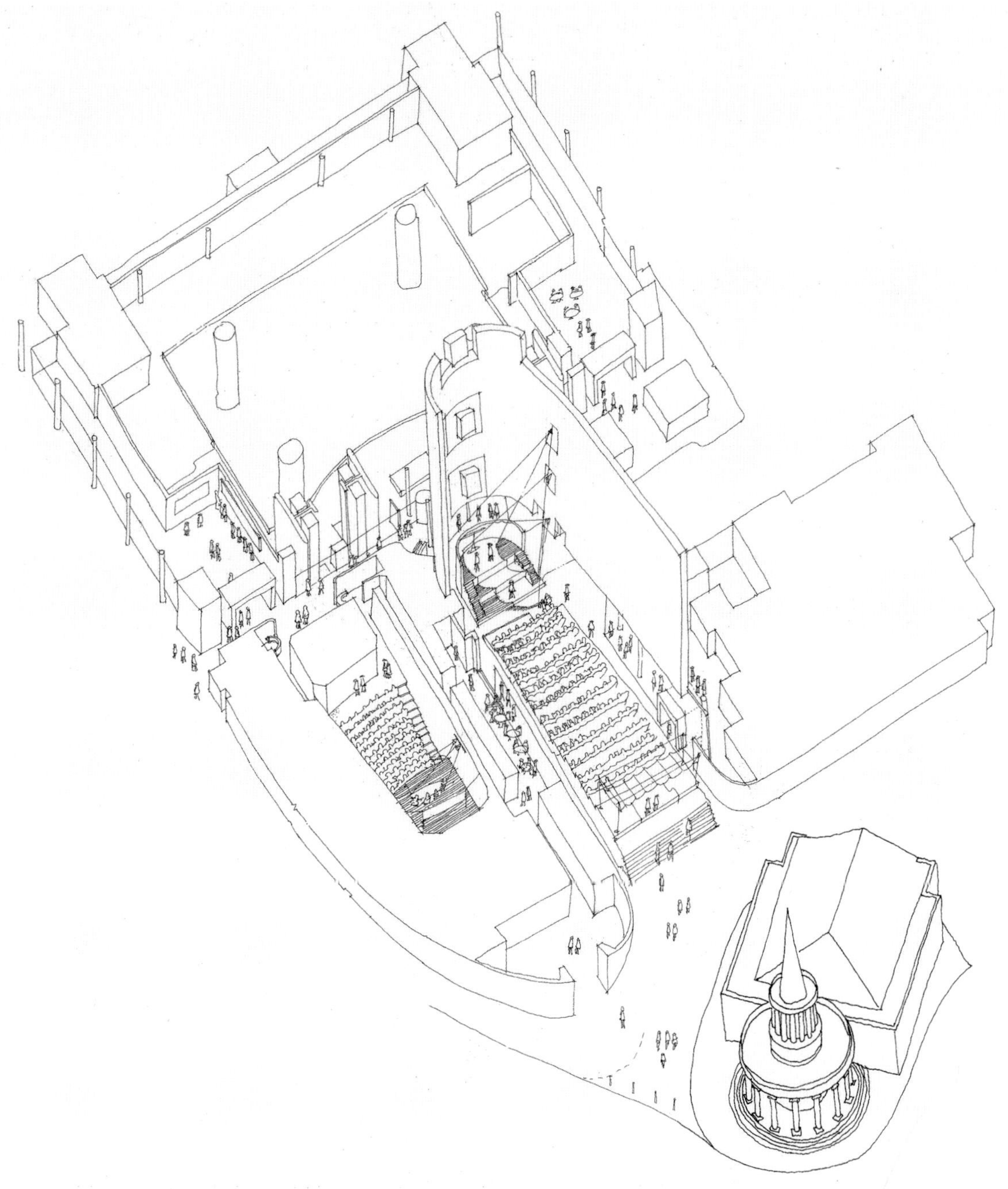

17

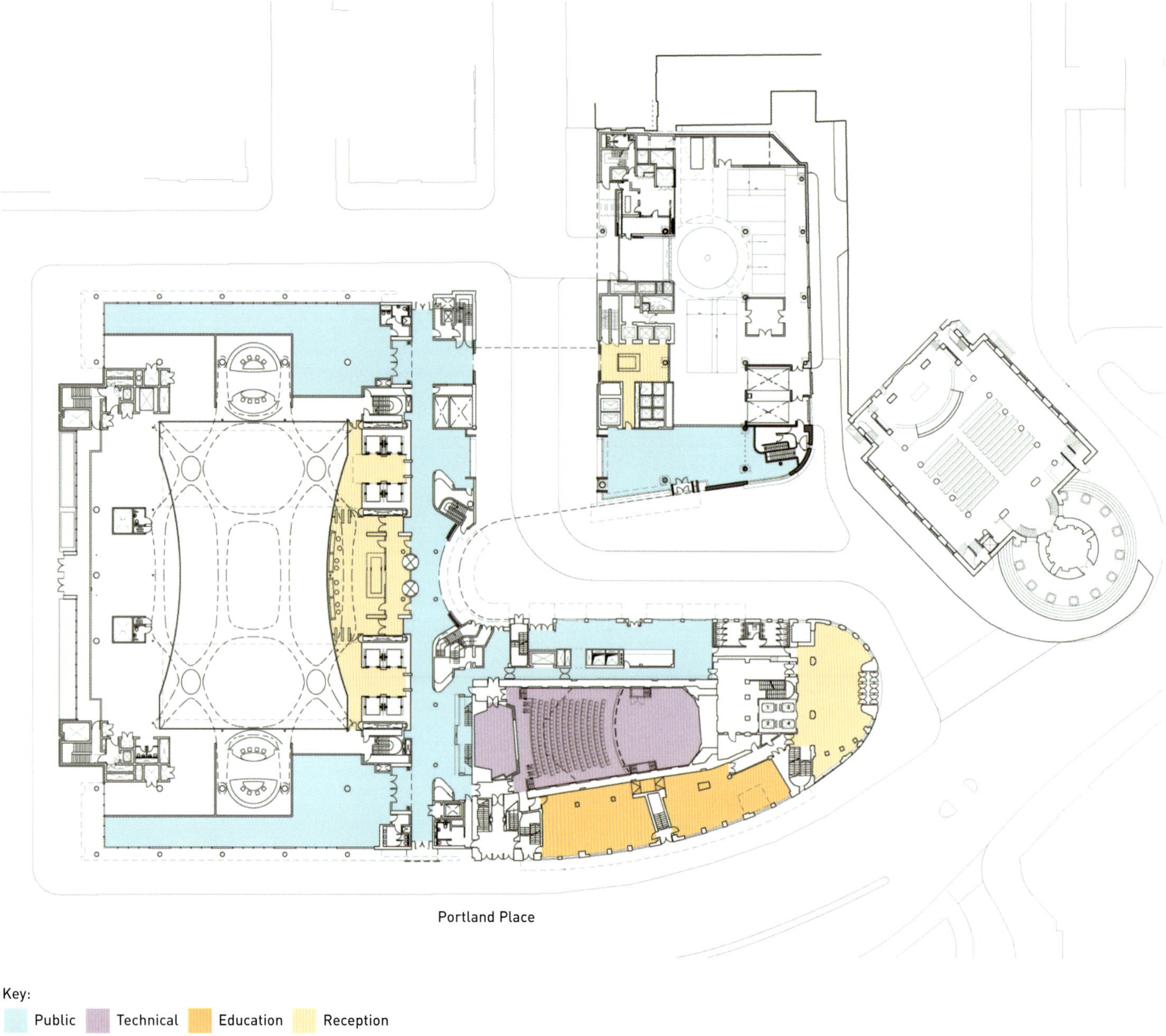

Portland Place

Key:
Public Technical Education Reception

18

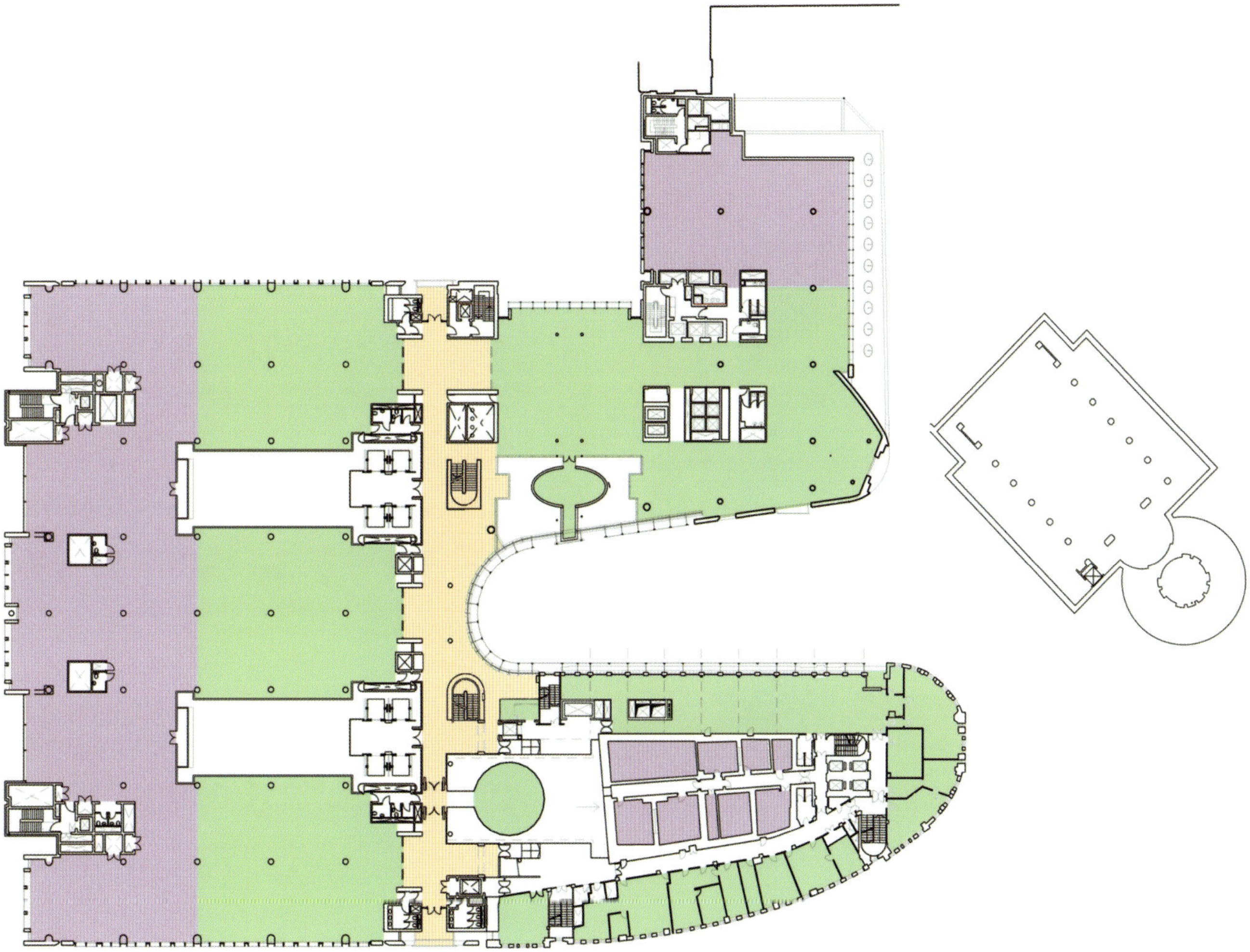

Key:
Technical Production Thoroughfare

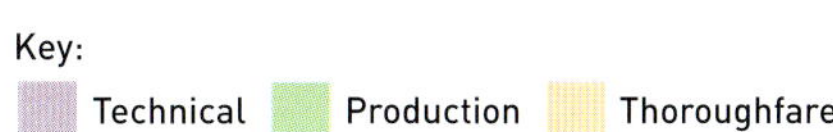

19

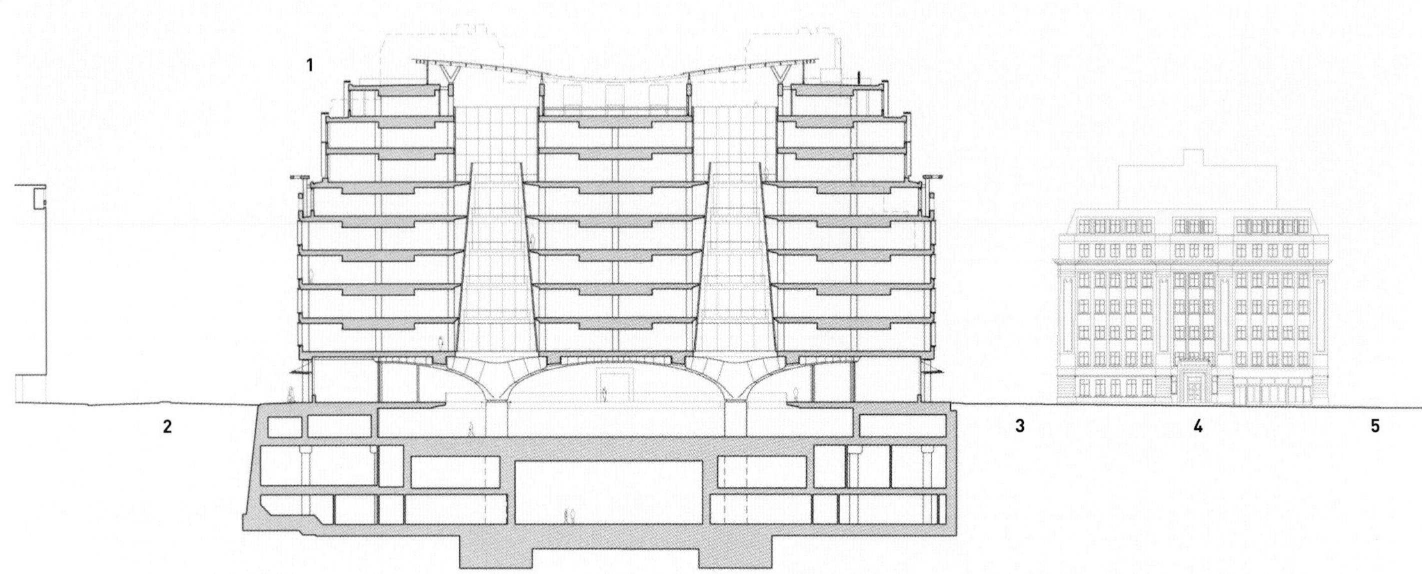

Alongside the Langham Street space, the undercroft of the new bridge link building provides a covered drop-off point for arrivals by car, taxi or shuttle bus from White City. The bridge will act as a threshold between the grand scale of Regent Street and Portland Place and the rich diversity of the streetscape in East Marylebone. It also provides visual enclosure, which is needed to establish the new public space.

The Langham Street elevation of BH is currently constrained because of the five-storey catslide roof that was a last-minute alteration to Val Myer's design in response to complaints about reduced light from the residents opposite. Val Myer clearly wanted to hide the roof from Regent Street and concealed it behind the upper storeys of the curved front, sacrificing the symmetry he had had in the original 'Top Hat' scheme. MJP is removing this roof and creating larger floor plates for new operational accommodation. This will also result in the reinstating of the ring of offices around the upper levels of the building that were so integral to Val Myer's original plan. Roof set-backs at seventh-floor level will reduce the scale of the new extension. The new floors replacing those under the catslide roof will be glazed. The outer face of glass will be textured with an interlayer of white fritting and etched so that, in daylight hours, it will form a non-reflective white surface complementing the Portland stone at the lower level.

The facades of the new extension will become a giant art work in their own right. Much time and energy is being spent on developing the transparency and opacity of the glass that will change during the day and night and act as a foil to the Portland stone and steel. The partly curved screen hung in front

17 Ground floor plan.

18 Typical upper floor plan.

19 East-west section.
Key:
1 Outline to existing BHX building (to be demolished)
2 Portland Place
3 Hallam Street
4 Western House
5 Great Portland Street

20 North-south section.
Key:
1 Duchess Street
2 BH
3 All Souls' Place

20

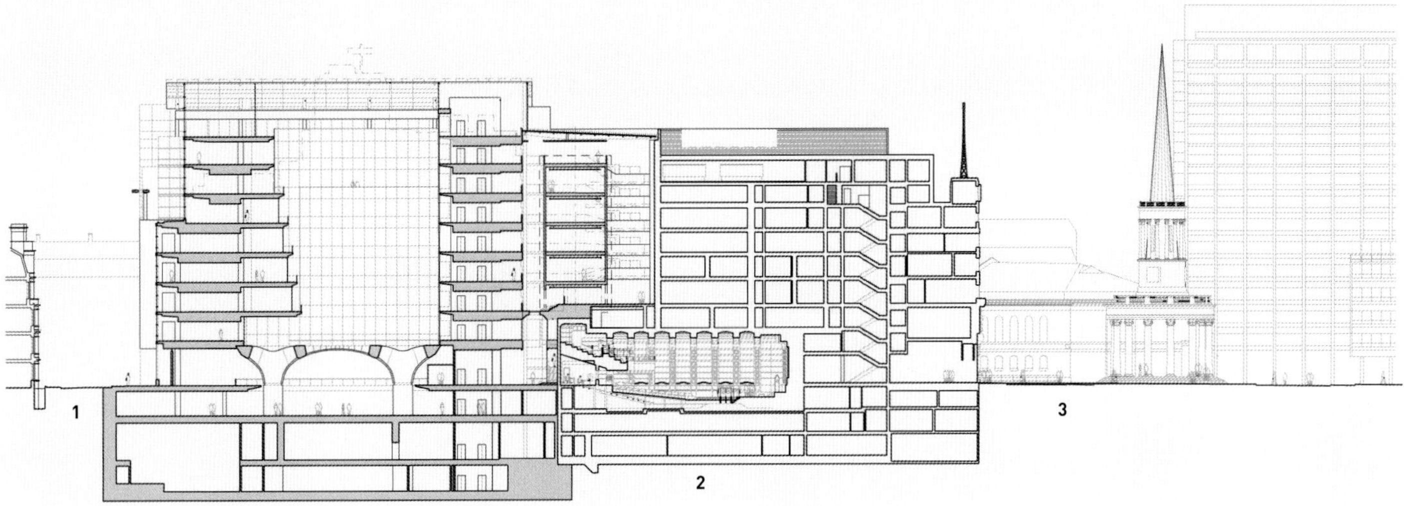

of the north end of the outdoor space will offer glimpses inside the building while providing continuity of form. Most importantly, from an urban point of view, the drum and spire of All Souls church will have a symmetrical backdrop when viewed from Oxford Circus.

The north-west elevation of All Souls, currently out of view, will become an important part of the new scheme. The public space will be augmented by an arcade running the width of the site, from Portland Place to Hallam Street, providing new access to the Radio Theatre and allowing the public deep within the building without creating a security risk. The arcade will include a new staff entrance and reception area, internet education area, café, shop, cloakrooms and ticket counters and a new foyer for the Radio Theatre, as well as being a short-cut for residents and workers until after evening performances in the theatre. Broadcasting House will not only be open in a way it has never been before, it will actively be encouraging Londoners and visitors to use the public spaces around and within it. It will become a vital and vibrant part of the urban fabric rather than merely a handsome landmark.

Within the new BH, Richard MacCormac has seized the opportunity to provide chance meeting places and a sense of orientation within the building. 'The idea is that you work formally in the production areas and elsewhere is an interstitial territory that's highly social and interactive, and spatially very exciting, with good views so that people can be seen in the lifts and on the stairs.' Cross circulation provides views north and south across the atria and out into Portland Place and Langham Street. This will orientate people in relation to the rest of the building and the city outside. The staircases – on which many key decisions are apparently made – are left open. 'It was crucial that we negotiate that', says MacCormac, 'as it's so important to the scheme.' The double-height cafeterias interlock with double-height quadrants, or break-out spaces, on alternate floors that result in 'terrific diagonal views up and down through all the social spaces'. Attention has been paid to details such as the special handrails on the landings, which have been designed to encourage people to put down laptops or files and encourage conversation in passing.

Throughout the design process MacCormac has come back to the idea of interstitial space, what he also calls 'shorelines', confident in the metaphorical idea that 'the richest ecological situations are at the interstices between different ecologies, on the edge of a wood or valley, or by the sea. So where different

21 Birds-eye view down Langham Street, with BH to the left and the hotch-potch of 1960s additions behind and to the side.

22 Computer image of the MJP scheme as it will look on completion. The recognisable entrance of the existing BH, with its Gill sculpture, clock and radio aerial is retained. The unsightly Egton House building is entirely redesigned in sympathy with the existing BH and the scooped out space in between functions as a way of inviting the public in and providing extra space for BBC and public activity.

21

22

"societies" or groups come together should be highly interactive.' It is an evocative and highly visual image and one that Broadcasting House, the moored ocean liner at the top of Regent Street, is eminently suited to.

The BBC is a creative organisation, the product of which is television and radio programmes. But unlike conventional 'manufacturers', it is not usually possible to see the process by which the product is made. Efforts are being made in all the new buildings to show visitors studio spaces and dispel much of the mystery of the BBC. What it will never be able to show is the thinking process – the hours of debate and discussion that go into each episode of every television or radio series. The new buildings need to stimulate that process, and MacCormac and his team have kept this need at the forefront of their minds from the beginning. Rather like at architecture school, explains MacCormac, you can't quantify what is going on in people's minds. 'One sort of environment I know about is academic buildings, where people sit around on beanbags and discuss ideas. The BBC is a rather upmarket version of that!'

At the heart of the building sits the giant newsroom, the largest of its kind anywhere in the world at 4120 square metres. Situated at ground and lower ground floor level to allow for maximum uninterrupted floorspace, the whole weight of the building is drawn down onto the branches of huge tree-like transfer columns, with a circumference of 9562 millimetres. This structure enables the centre of the newsroom to be column-free. It will be glimpsed from inside the building and staff and visitors will literally be able to see the news in action. The potential claustrophobia of working below ground level will be avoided

23 

23 Computer image of the MJP scheme showing the view from Portland Place.

by flooding the space with daylight from the two atria above.

The open, bustling environment of the newsroom will be emulated throughout the building, in what MacCormac describes as a workshop environment. 'We've provided 40 per cent studio-capable space, which means that the loadings are twice normal office loadings, across the north of the main building, and that can provide an impressive number of studios which everyone is pretty close to', he explains. His practice will also be responsible for all the interior design. MacCormac took some of the senior BBC personnel to the practice's award-winning Wellcome Wing at the Science Museum and they were impressed by the industrial aesthetic. Where possible, ceilings in the new Broadcasting House will be left exposed and services will be articulated.

With lifts at the centre of the circulation system and links to secondary circulation at every level via the main thoroughfare, MJP has ensured legibility throughout the new extension. Facilities will be shared and departmental front doors will face onto the main thoroughfares, with decision-makers' offices accessible.

George Orwell, who worked for the BBC from August 1941 for the Eastern Service, described Broadcasting House as 'something halfway between a girls' school and a lunatic asylum'; indeed the interiors provided the inspiration for the infamous and hellish Room 101, in his novel *1984*. Who knows which literary figures will draw inspiration from MJP's Broadcasting House? What is certain is that it will provide some of the most inspiring and dramatic spaces in London, for BBC employees and the public alike. Orwell would be lost for words, were he alive to see it.

24 Computer image of what will be the largest newsroom of its kind in the world. The entire weight of the building is drawn down onto the branches of huge tree-like columns. This allows the centre of the newsroom to be column-free, releasing the maximum amount of space. The newsroom will be viewed from above, and will be flooded with daylight from the two atria.

25+26 Studies by MJP showing the view of BH from Oxford Circus at different times of day.

27 Photos of a model showing the effect of natural and artificial light on the curved glass screen of the Langham Street façade. Much time has been spent on developing the colour and opacity of the glass which will change during the day and night and act as a foil to the Portland stone and steel. The screen will offer glimpses inside the building while providing continuity of form.

25

26

27

5

TELEVISION CENTRE

2 The envelope addressed to Miss Alice Bridge at Wood House, thought to be the farmhouse that stood on the site of TVC in the nineteenth century.

3 View from a balloon of the Franco-British exhibition of 1908 in London's Shepherd's Bush.

4 In 1949 the BBC acquired 13.5 acres of land, occupied by the 1908 Court of Honour (shown here at night), for its television factory (Television Centre).

5 Several other exhibitions were held on the site. Shown here, The Witching Waves from the Imperial International Exhibition of 1909.

6 View from the Canadian Pavilion at the 1908 exhibition.

2

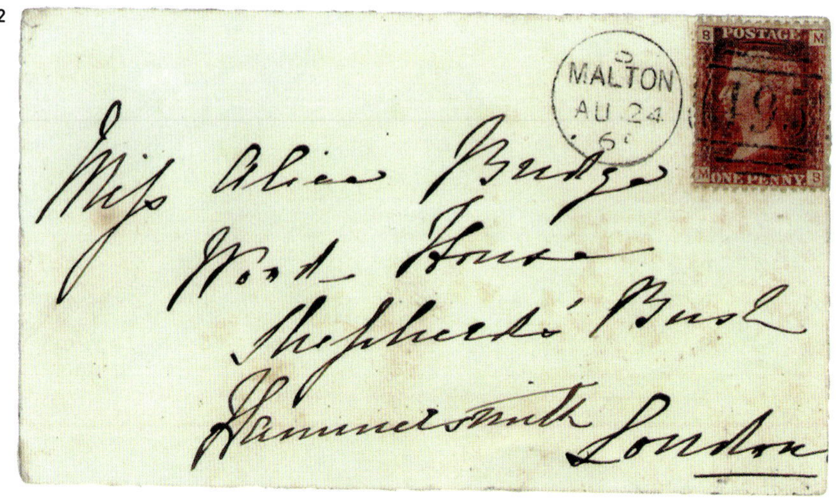

Television Centre is in Shepherd's Bush, W12. Until 1900, sheep grazed on the Bush common on their way to Smithfield market. The BBC's written archive in Caversham has an envelope addressed to Miss Alice Bridge, Wood House, Shepherd's Bush, Hammersmith, London, dated 24 August 1869. It is assumed that this was the farmhouse that stood on the site of Television Centre. We know that almost 40 years later 140 acres of land in the area was used as part of the exhibition site for the Franco-British exhibition of 1908 – eight times the size of Hyde Park's 1851 exhibition. The event was suggested by the London branch of the French chamber of commerce, a joint exhibition to display industrial and cultural achievements by the two countries. In 1906, while it was being planned, Britain was invited to host the 1908 Olympics. The Italians had failed to raise the money to build an Olympic Stadium in Rome so, at the eleventh hour, a stadium was incorporated into the White City complex.

Twenty palaces and 120 exhibition buildings linked by roads and bridges were constructed by a workforce of some 12,000 men. The most impressive attraction was a precursor to today's British Airways London Eye: the flip-flap machine. It had two 45 metre long arms and carriages from which you could see London 60 metres below. Several temporary 'villages', including an Irish and Sengalese example complete with imported residents, were built alongside a reconstruction of old London and a *Daily Mail* newsroom. All the buildings were constructed of steel frames and concrete with ornate mouldings fixed onto them, to lend an air of opulence. The buildings were then whitewashed to protect them against the weather, giving rise to the name 'White City'. The exhibition closed on 31 October 1908. Some £420,000 was taken on the gate through which 8,400,000 people passed.

Several other exhibitions were held on the site, including the Japan-British exhibition of 1910 and the Coronation exhibition the following year. The British Industries fair exhibited for two to three weeks a year from 1921 until 1929, and before that the war department used the larger buildings on the site to build aeroplanes. On 7 November 1922, White City was put up for auction. The Holborn Empire Company's failure to follow through its bid for the site saw White City return to exhibition use – as a venue for textile fairs – until 1937. During the Second World War much of the site was commandeered for the manufacture of parachutes, an operation that required the cavernous spaces of the exhibition halls. Afterwards, some of the large spaces were used for the construction of

3

Copyright by Wakefield Ealing W.
6791 W
FRANCO-BRITISH EXHIBITION.
BIRDS-EYE VIEW FROM BALLOON.
ROTARY PHOTO, E.C.

4

In Court of Honour at Night,
Franco-British Exhibition, London, 1908.
VALENTINE'S SERIES. COPYRIGHT.

5

THE WITCHING WAVES.
IMPERIAL INTERNATIONAL EXHIBITION, LONDON, 1909
VALENTINE'S SERIES. COPYRIGHT.

6

View from Canadian Pavilion, The Great White City, London
SCENIC RAILWAY
NOTICE
437
VALENTINE'S SERIES. COPYRIGHT.

7 Aerial view of TVC showing the large circular building around a 150-foot courtyard, surrounded by studios and enclosed by a scenery runway, at around the time of opening in 1960.

8 Axonometric projection of TVC. The tail of the question mark formation is an extension of the scenery runway.

7

television and film scenery. Then in 1949 the BBC acquired 13.5 acres of land, occupied by the Court of Honour at the original Franco-British exhibition, for its television factory. A metre square of tiles outside Studio 1 is the only surviving reminder of the 1908 exhibition.

The search for a suitable home for a new television centre was spurred on by the expiry of the lease at Alexandra Palace in 1956. At the time, a 25-acre site at White City was the largest single undeveloped site in the capital and the BBC acquired just over half of it. On 15 November 1949, the BBC's Board of Governors selected Graham Dawbarn of Norman and Dawbarn Architects to work on the project with BBC Chief Civil Engineer, Marmaduke T Tudsbery (as G Val Myer had done on Broadcasting House). Sir Howard M Robertson and Sir William J Holford were architectural consultants on the project.

The question mark formation of Dawbarn's original sketch consisted of a large circular building around a 150-foot courtyard, surrounded by studios and enclosed by a 'scenery runway'. The tail of the question mark, or 'spur', is an extension of the runway to the west of it. The blocks for scenery, offices and restaurant are grouped around the main building. The studios are enveloped by a ring road to allow easy access for equipment through double-height doors. Provision was made for a second channel, BBC2, and for the extra technical space that would be required for colour television. The concept was intended to facilitate rapid studio turnaround – the ability to use every studio, every day by striking and resetting the scenery overnight. Planning permission was granted on 28 June 1950, and work began soon afterwards. In 1951 a model of the scheme was exhibited at the Royal Academy, and another model shown at the Festival of Britain. By the end of that year Dawbarn and Tudsbery had drawn up a 50-page brief.

Delays to the project occurred from April 1951 to the end of 1953 due to Government limitations on capital expenditure as a result of the high cost of the Korean War. While all this was going on, the Television Service had expanded into the old Gaumont film studios at Lime Grove, and the temporary Riverside Studios at Hammersmith. Lessons learned there were taken into account in the developing design at Television Centre. Simple things, such as the sizes and aspect ratios of the studios, the advantages of separate production, vision and sound control rooms, and the highly flexible lighting systems were pioneered here by the BBC. They have since become common features of the world's television

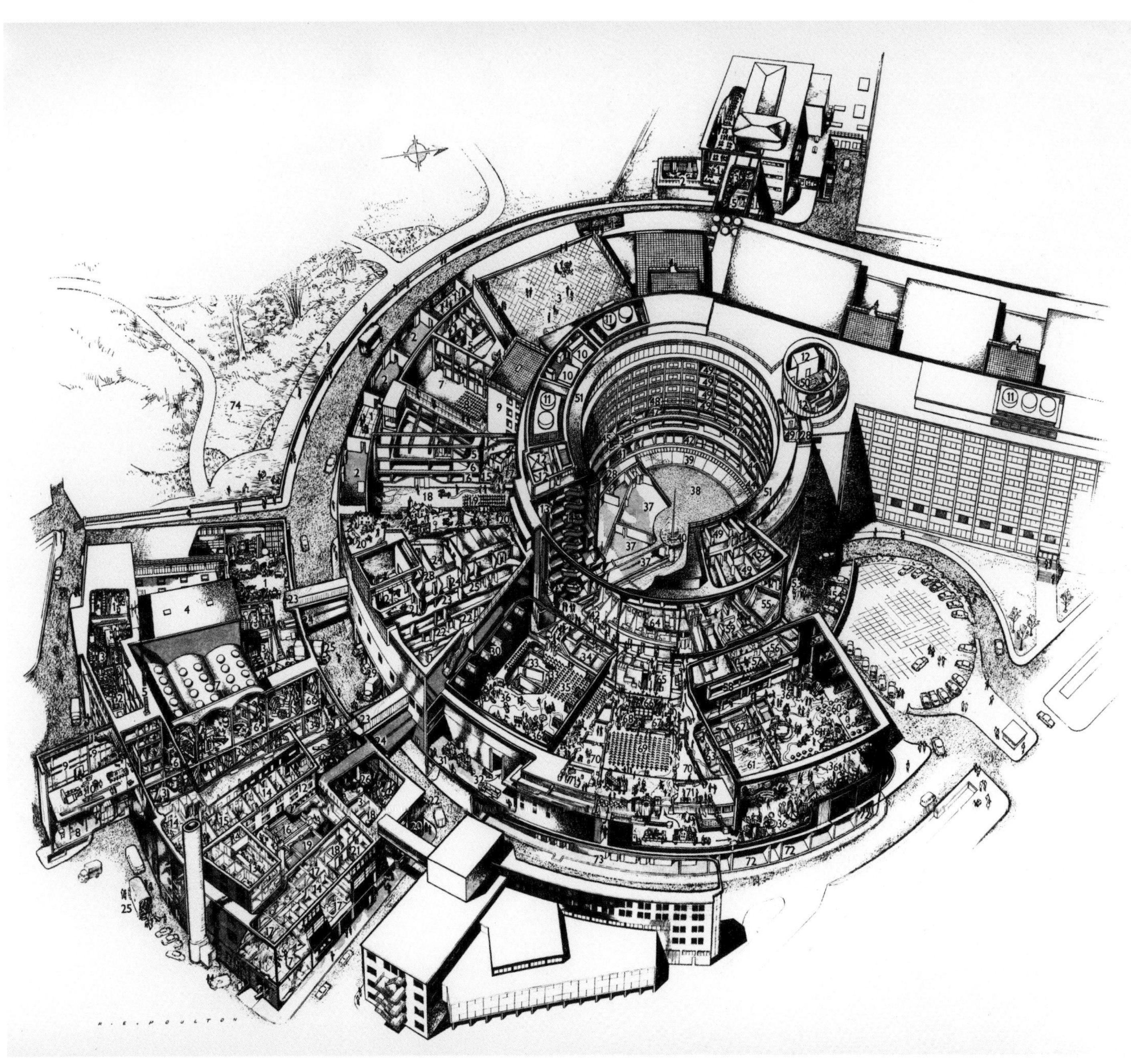
H. E. POULTON

9

9 View of the original main reception at TVC.

10 Aerial view of the central courtyard with the fountain by TB Huxley-Jones with a three-metre high gilded bronze figure of Helios.

facilities. However, not every innovation was a success. Three of the major studios were constructed with the ability to remove part of the floor, exposing a huge water tank below. The tank structures still exist but unfortunately no one was able to design removable floor panels that, when replaced, would be flat enough to track cameras on. For many years, the tank below TC1 housed Television Centre's telephone exchange.

The project had been divided into three initial stages (and a further three followed later). Stage 3 was not completed until 1960 at a cost – for the whole project – of £10m. When it opened, the press applauded loudly. Manchester's *Evening Chronicle* declared: 'What Hollywood is to the film industry the new BBC Television Centre in London will become to television – the world's largest producer of programmes ... It also happens to be one of the pleasantest factories imaginable to work in.' Dawbarn and Tudsbery must have been happy about the industrial reference. It is clear that they had not intended to build an iconic work of architecture. In a press release they claimed that it was 'a means to an end, to be planned and constructed to satisfy the particular requirements of those who use it'.

As at Broadcasting House, artists were employed to work at Television Centre. The centrepiece of the circular courtyard is a fountain by TB Huxley-Jones. A 3 metre high gilded bronze figure of Helios, the sun god of Greek mythology, sits atop a freestanding bowl supported on four legs. Below the bowl is a pool in which two reclining figures, representing vision and sound, are seated on raised plinths. Sadly, the fountain caused too much distraction to the workers in the offices overlooking the courtyard and water began to leak into the basement recording area. As a result, Helios and his friends have remained dry since shortly after the opening of Television Centre. Inside, for the west wall opposite the entrance doors to the original reception area (now known as Stage Door), another fine work of art was commissioned. The abstract mural in vibrant colours, by John Piper (see chapter 9), uses vitreous glass, ceramic and porcelain from Italy, Sweden and India.

Stage 4 – the spur – was completed after the grand opening of 1960 and built to house BBC Television News, at the time still operating from Alexandra Palace. The extension provided two news studios and provision for film processing and transmission, as well as an eighth large production studio to complement the seven already in use. The building, which was completed at a cost of £1m, was gradually occupied during the autumn of 1964. BBC

10

11 

12 

Television News did not move into its new home until September 1969. But still the building work continued. In 1978 plans were made for an extension to accommodate a Television Theatre together with a new videotape facility for 100 broadcast-quality machines and accommodation for staff from Lime Grove. Other projects, including the EBX block by the BBC Architectural and Civil Engineering Department and a multistorey car park, were completed before the foundations of Stage 5 were laid in 1985. It was completed in 1988. Bill Cotton, Managing Director Television, declared it 'the beginning of the finishing of Television Centre'. He spoke 10 years too soon.

Stage 6 marked the final stage of Television Centre's development to date, completed 50 years after that first sketch by Graham Dawbarn. The News Centre is home to 1200 television and radio news staff and was opened

11 Radio News team in Newsroom, Stage 6, TVC; a far cry from what they will enjoy when relocated to the state of the art accommodation at Broadcasting House.

12 TVC Newsroom Two Desk in 1970 with newsreader Peter Woods sitting second from the left.

THEATRE 1
RINGMAIN-Mono
THEATRE 2
RINGMAIN-Colour
HOLD

13 Alan Yentob, Director, Drama, Entertainment and Children, in his office in Television Centre designed by DEGW. Yentob describes TVC as 'a work in progress'.

14 The open plan offices on the sixth floor of TVC for the controllers of the television networks, designed by Amalgam and design company Lucy or Robert.

13

by Chairman Sir Christopher Bland in July 1998. The four-storey building opens onto Wood Lane and now houses the main reception, which is dominated by Henry Moore's Reclining Figure: Hand, on loan from the Henry Moore Foundation. Significant improvements have been made to some of the offices within Television Centre, including Alan Yentob's office by DEGW and the open-plan offices on the sixth floor of the spur for the controllers of the television networks by Amalgam. Television Centre is, as Alan Yentob describes it, 'a work in progress'. It is essentially a fine building which has been spoiled by ill-considered additions such as Stage 6 and the East Tower. John Smith's ambition is to restore it to Grade 1 listed status.

Television Centre has a rich history but its development has not been straightforward; nor is it over yet. Until the mid-1990s, all the studios were in constant use. Chris Evans, Project Director for Broadcasting House, affectionately describes the building as 'a bonkers place. Even if you weren't a programme maker you felt part of it. There was once a greyhound race around the fourth-floor corridor and I remember watching Bill Oddie leaping off the East Tower one day, and on another occasion seeing a helicopter swoop down to deliver cheques [to game-show contestants].'

Then, in 1993 the BBC introduced 'Producer Choice', which meant that studio users were free to use independent as well as BBC studios. At the same time there was a shift away from studio-based dramas and the Saturday night shows. 'For a while that meant that the studios kind of died. It had a significant effect on the atmosphere and community of TVC', says Evans.

When Greg Dyke became Director-General, he questioned the logic of leaving studios empty in Television Centre while renting cheaper facilities elsewhere. He has instigated a move back into Television Centre. *Top of the Pops* has returned from Elstree and some of the buzz has been injected back into the community. 'The theatre of the place is what makes it edgy', says Evans. 'Those who say that big studio production will soon die [at the hands of virtual reality studios and laptop production] are talking tosh. All the presenters, even for news, have to work with the live camera, not with visual trickery. Tension is part of the theatre and it's the same for producers as presenters – they all thrive on it.'

When News moves to Broadcasting House in 2006, more space will be freed up within Television Centre to make it once more the home of studio-based drama and entertainment.

14

15

15 The Blue Peter garden, complete with Goldie, one of the most familiar sights at TVC.

6

WHITE CITY

1 The original White City building by Scott Brownrigg Turner has been variously described as a 'tin shed' and 'silver brick'. It is an inward looking building which pays little respect to the surrounding housing estate and school and which has proved difficult and expensive to reconfigure internally.

WHITE CITY

The failure of the BBC to build the much-publicised Foster scheme for Langham Place in the 1980s resulted in the construction of one of the most universally hated properties in its portfolio. This was largely brought about by a change of guard at the Corporation. In 1983 Stuart Young had replaced George Howard as Chairman and initiated a feasibility study for the potential use of the dog track site at White City, using the sale of the Langham island site as part of the equity, as explained in Chapter 3.

This was a property that looked in on itself, turning its back on its neighbours and providing little in the way of a stimulating environment. Architecturally it was, and still is, a disaster: a dismal, characterless building where design quality was subjugated to cost efficiency. John Smith describes it as BBC Property's architectural 'nadir' and few would disagree. Despite the impressive volume of the building, it has proved difficult and fantastically expensive to reconfigure as often as is required.

Looking back, it defies belief that anyone should have believed that such a process could have resulted in a new headquarters to rival Broadcasting House. Although it was intended to be the administrative headquarters, and housed offices for some of the central directorates, as well as a little-used boardroom and several meeting rooms, it never took the place of BH.

Since its completion in 1990, several studies have considered how the site might be further developed. All were abandoned through lack of interest or funding. Plans for turning the new building into the home of radio and news were dropped in the early 1990s. Then, in 1997 George Crowe, (Controller of Property from 1993 to 2002), raised an issue that led to the rebirth of White City. Crowe reminded his colleagues that the lease on Bush House would expire in 2008, so a new property strategy for London had to be considered. John Birt commissioned a project team led by Tony Hall (then Director, News and Current Affairs) with John Smith, who took the helm after Hall's departure to the Royal Opera House. With Greg Dyke's arrival as Director-General in 1999, Smith also took over the BBC's entire property operation. Staff numbers had expanded significantly with the advent of the new digital services and the extraordinary growth of the Online team to more than 1000 employees.

After three years of workshops, feasibility studies and negotiation, a strategy was finally settled in early 2000. It was decided to radically rationalise the estate in London and reduce the 30 or so sites to three. Broadcasting House would be redeveloped to produce the largest

1

2

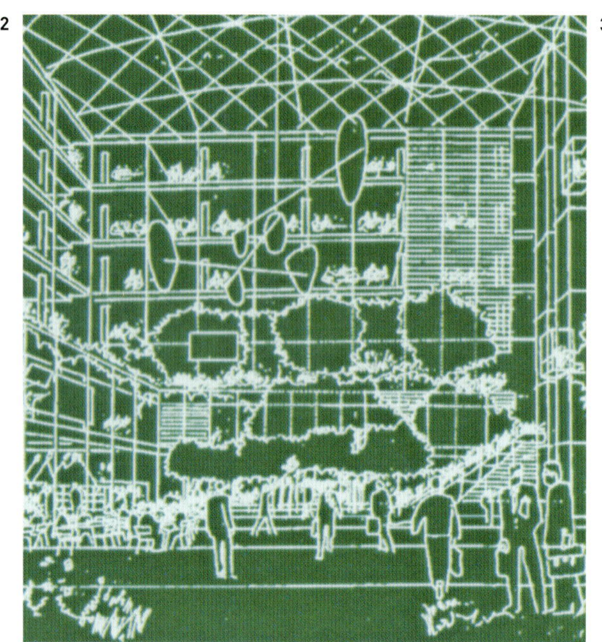

3

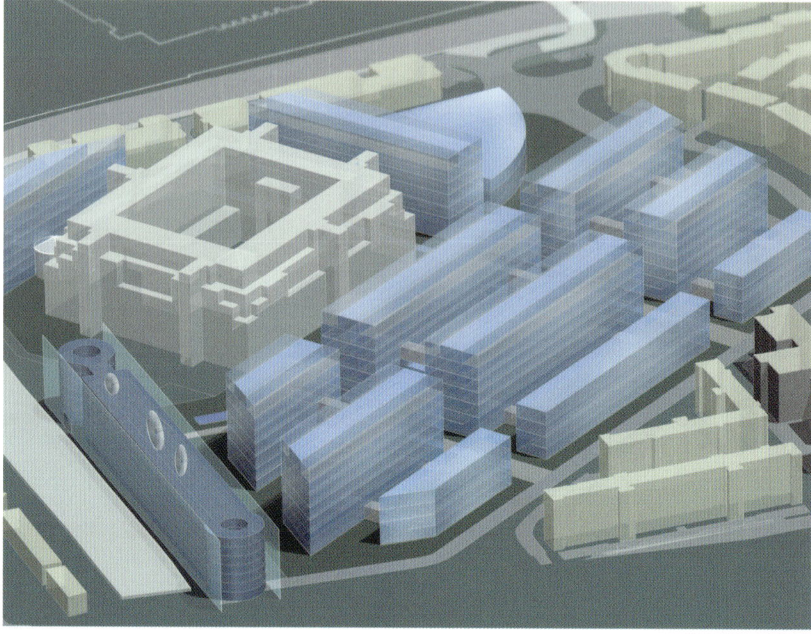

live broadcasting centre in the world, uniting all the BBC's network radio channels, the 40 languages of the World Service and all the network news journalism across television and radio. Television Centre would be restored to its original purpose: a television factory producing hits from *Top of the Pops* to *Blue Peter*. White City would then become a mixed media campus.

Perhaps the most significant move by John Smith and the property team at this stage was to call in two outside advisers: Sir Stuart Lipton and Ricky Burdett, both of whom were subsequently involved on Broadcasting House. A competition to develop the White City media campus, before the new strategy was in place, had pitched three commercial firms against one another: epr, Aukett and RMJM. Lipton and Burdett did not pull any punches when asked to respond to the three entries. Part of the problem had been with the client's brief. The competition was disbanded and another one mounted, under the guidance of a panel who oversaw the selection process and steered the design as it evolved. This was the first of many projects handled in this way. Invited architects, Allies and Morrison, Ian Ritchie Architects and John McAslan and Partners, were given a short, non-technical brief written by Burdett with Ian Robertson, BBC in-house architect Alan James and Roger Ackroyd who, as Development Manager, has played a key role throughout and provided direction to the design team.

This time the BBC was determined to get it right. The strategic intent for the buildings needed to be developed before producing a brief and selecting architects. The commissioning team was formed to plan and run the competition process with military

2 Competition scheme for the new White City by John McAslan and Partners.

3 Ian Ritchie Architects' competition scheme.

4 Main entrance to the Central Office building, showing the internal 'artwall'.

4

5

6

precision. Lipton and Burdett were treated as insiders with the same goals and aspirations as the BBC directors. Lipton was particularly impressed by the BBC team's 'open and interested' response to the advisers' ideas. 'It was clear that there was a desire to do something which was effective, efficient and aesthetically challenging. This happens elsewhere. What was unusual in this case was the amount of care taken during the process.'

Lipton and Burdett also witnessed the breadth and depth of participation by senior BBC directors and the tangible enthusiasm for the project. Lipton's experience as a developer who has always recognised 'the value of art to the value of business' on projects such as Broadgate gave the BBC the confidence it needed to take some of the more apparently risky decisions, particularly when it came to Broadcasting House. The collaborative effort of client, contractor, architect and artists results in buildings that cost less and deliver more. It works, he says, 'if you're upfront about everything and don't pretend that cost isn't a parameter'.

Each entry underwent forensic examination of its efficiency, aesthetic qualities and contribution to the surrounding community. From the beginning John Smith needed little persuasion of the benefits of good design and was often the one pushing hardest for a clear architectural vision.

Competition winners Bob Allies and Graham Morrison were also struck by the BBC's approach. 'We had only about a month to do the competition and the client came to see us during the process, which although unusual was helpful and encouraging', says Bob Allies. Very quickly, the pair realised that their job was to be an exercise in planning as much as architecture. 'We looked at building urban blocks, and then broke it down into individual buildings.' Unlike the existing block, described by the architects as 'isolated and pompous', the three buildings of Allies and Morrison's first phase have been designed to engage with users both within and outside the BBC. A street the width of Oxford Street runs between the original building and the new development and will incorporate retail and catering facilities at ground level. Additional buildings on the perimeter, to be occupied by independent businesses, will introduce a break in scale and address the surrounding streets to ensure a safe, friendly environment.

BBC Project Director Tony Wilson believes the challenge for the team is 'to persuade nearly 3000 staff based in W1, who are used to all the benefits that W1 has to offer, that moving to White City will be

7

8

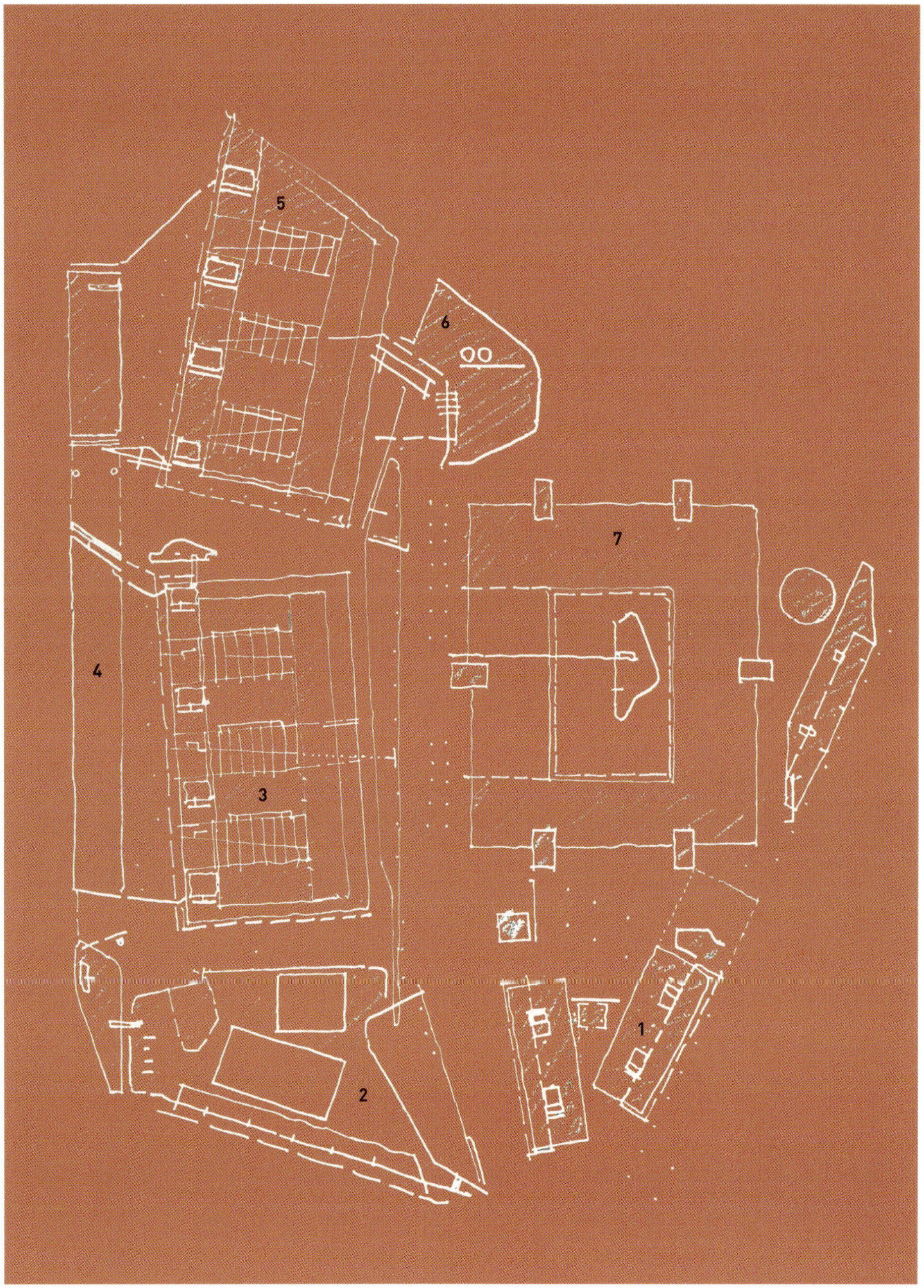

5 Model of the Allies and Morrison scheme with the Broadcast Centre in the foreground. Perimeter office buildings shown to the right, in white.

6 Model showing a glimpse of the existing building through the gap between the Broadcast Centre (left) and the Central Office Building (right).

7 Aerial view of model.

8 Corresponding drawing. The two largest buildings share a similar plan of four 'arms' of floor space, each 18 metres deep, arranged around three roof-lit atria.
Key:
1 Entrance building
2 Music Centre
3 Central Office Building
4 Perimeter buildings
5 Broadcast Centre
6 Energy Centre
7 Existing building

9 Site plan submitted for planning approval, December 2000.

10 Computer image of how the completed scheme will look. The M40 runs past the Broadcast Centre and Energy Centre. The housing estate and school are in the foreground. The Music Centre to the far right will be designed by an architect of international renown, not yet announced at the time of going to press.

9

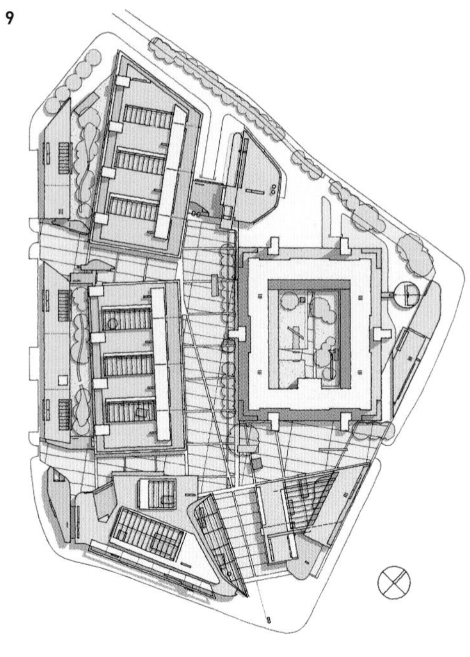

a positive experience for them. Within the new public space, we will have some of the life and activity that you expect to find in Oxford Street, so that W12 will no longer be considered an inferior location to W1.' The design team is considering how best to improve and update the existing building, as well as design the very best new facilities.

Uppermost in the minds of both client and architect has been the need to maximise flexibility within the plan and steer clear of a corporate campus. 'Our brief was for the buildings to have a long life and a loose fit. The straightforward design allows for more focus on the spaces in between. We're designing the spaces and the environment as much as the buildings', say Allies and Morrison.

The landscape design for the new public spaces is by Christopher Bradley-Hole. He too has been concerned with improving the environment around the existing building as well as focusing on the new spaces. He was inspired by the architect's solution of creating a site that invites interaction. His aim was to ensure that the architecture and landscape appear closely linked, an organic process of development such as you would get in a town or village. 'Bob and Graham talk about the normality of the scheme, and the idea is that there should be streets, not squares or piazzas.' The proportions and structural grids of the architecture are reflected and expressed within the landscape but at a subliminal level. There is a sense of progression and repetition that you would get in any street. 'There is an underlying proportion which as you walk through the space you'll feel, but I hope no one will worry about why. People should feel comfortable in the space, but there should also be some tension in it, a feeling that there is an edge to it', says Bradley-Hole.

Unlike most landscaping for corporate environments, Bradley-Hole has chosen deciduous trees, hedges with seasonal foliage and grasses and plants that change with the seasons. The formality of the planting loosens up towards the periphery of the site where trees will be left to grow naturally, in contrast to the clipped, boxy forms of the trees lining White City Place. Here hedges are kept low, for security, and the geometry is more ordered. Individual gardens relating to each of the new buildings are also designed by Bradley-Hole. The variations in formality, colour and planting help orientation within the site and provide different impressions of the overall landscape. A variety of paving materials helps to express the layers within the landscape. It reads as though the whole area was once paved in black granite out of which sections have been cut

10

11

11 Computer image showing the view from the M40. The Energy Centre may be enhanced by a video projection by artist Tim Head, working with Allies and Morrison and Bruce Kirk of Light Perceptions.

12

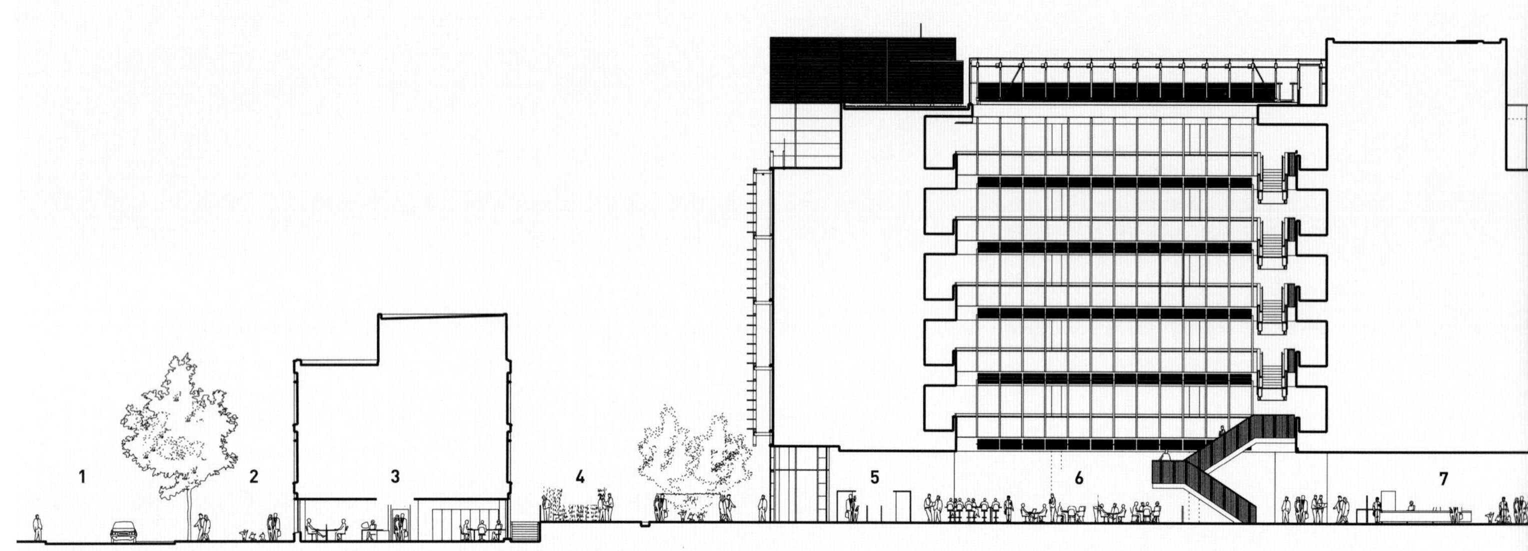

and infilled with concrete and other paving. There is also an area of suspended timber to bridge between the existing building and the new hard landscape. Four-inch deep recesses at soil-level are finished in compacted gravel. A pétanque area will provide entertainment in lunch breaks and overflowing pools will reflect the entrance to the Broadcast Centre.

White City will produce the first fruits of the partnership between the BBC and Land Securities Trillium. The total value of the groundbreaking deal is about £2bn, and there was a cash payment of £35m to the BBC on signing that went directly into programmes. The freehold for the BBC White City site has been transferred to the partnership and, as well as taking responsibility for implementation of the first phase at White City, LST will also provide property development and management of much of the BBC's estate for 30 years. LST delivers the essential finance, development and project management skills in response to the BBC's strategic property vision while the BBC retains design approval at every stage, and determines strategic priorities.

Despite being appointed by and working for the BBC in the initial phases, Allies and Morrison's 'client' is now the contractor, Bovis Lend Lease, who in turn is working for LST. Joanna Bacon, Allies and Morrison's Project Director, is enthusiastic about the collaborative nature of the project, although there were inevitable management changes to overcome. She also talks of a positive relationship with the planners. Peter Bishop, then director of Hammersmith and Fulham planning department, believed in the architect's strategy to reintegrate the site with the city. The current construction traffic and involvement with the local population, including the nearby school,

12 Section through the Central Office Building and existing building, linked by White City Place. Restaurants and gardens have been added to the existing building to ensure that it is integrated.
Key:
1 Parking
2 Garden
3 Perimeter building
4 Garden
5 Garden lobby
6 Atrium
7 Entrance foyer
8 White City Place
9 Moat
10 Restaurant
11 Servery
12 Courtyard
13 Café
14 Cloister
15 Garden

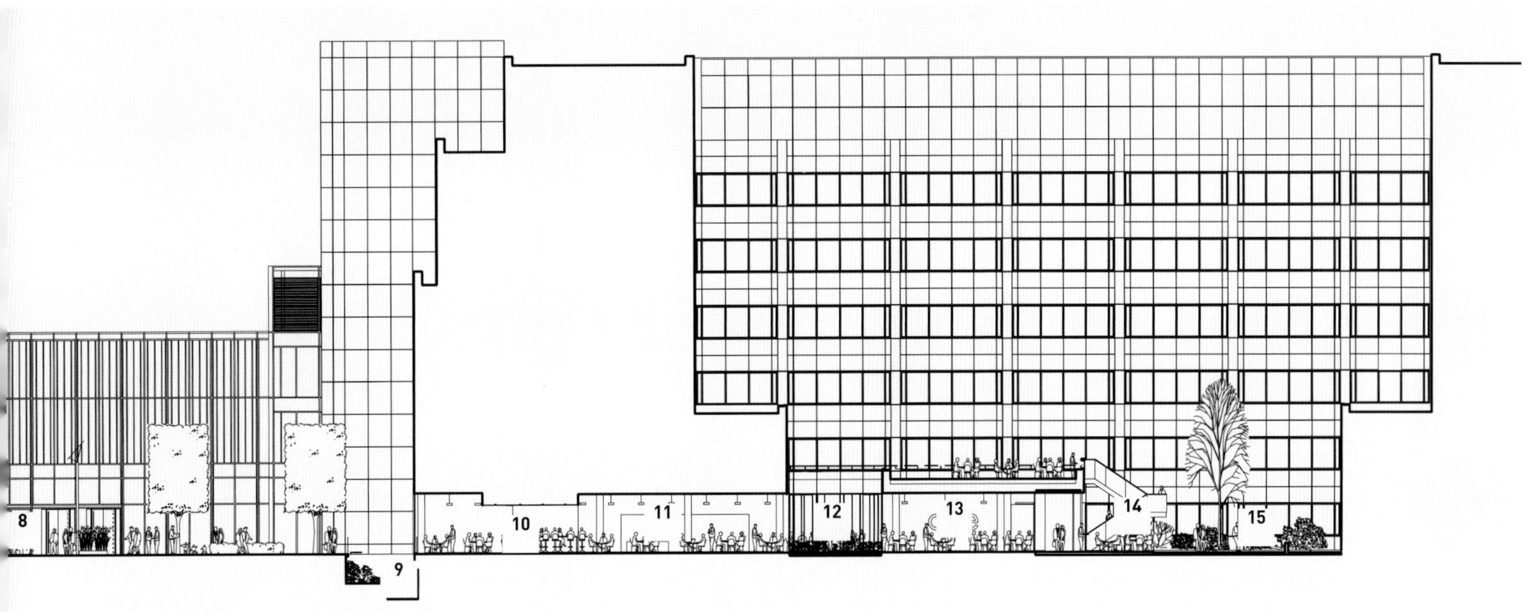

have already contributed to cleaning up the area and making it feel safer.

This is a fast-track project with completion of this phase scheduled for 2003, so the design discussions have been intense and tough. The new buildings lie to the west of the existing building: the Energy Centre (which will serve the entire site), the Broadcast Centre, with its complex technical core, and the Central Office Building containing 23,485 square metres of office and production space. The two largest buildings are clad in aluminium and glass with brises-soleil on the south and west elevations and opening shutters behind metal louvres wherever natural ventilation can be provided. These two buildings share a similar plan of four 'arms' of floor space, each 18 metres deep, arranged around three roof-lit atria. The atria promote visibility between individual offices and open up circulation between floors via the central staircases. One face of each atrium is left relatively open with glazed balustrades and a continuous walkway. The other is enclosed by timber panels.

Broadcasting House has often been referred to as an ocean liner sailing down Regent Street. Interestingly, Bob Allies' image for the interiors at White City is that of a ship, as expressed by the timber panels in the asymetrical atria, docking into the opposite, open facade, which is reached by stairs with a very gradual gradient. Allies and Morrison has also consciously emulated the loftiness and simplicity of warehouse spaces. While these White City buildings are heavily engineered and self-contained, they have a robustness and simplicity that are indicative of the architect's confidence. This is one of the largest and most significant projects yet for Allies and Morrison. Fortunately, it has avoided the temptation to cram the scheme with unnecessary detail and architectural fashion statements.

DEGW was part of the Land Securities Trillium bid for the project. The workspace specialist has been retained to work on the interiors at White City with Allies and Morrison, which retains sole control of the public areas. The working relationship has, by all accounts, been positive. DEGW has devised systems that will enable occupiers to personalise their spaces, such as a panel system that can be hooked on and off. By taking the ideas of scenery from studios, DEGW has given BBC employees something they can relate to. Terry Gunnery of DEGW talks of the need to reflect the building while still getting 'a sense of the media landscape and adding a discordant note, to make you think. It's a bit like city planning – it needs some less well-mannered interventions.' Allies and Morrison has ensured

13

13 The landscaping, by Christopher Bradley-Hole, is an essential component of the Allies and Morrison scheme. Shown here, the view onto White City Place from the existing building.

14 Computer image of view down White City Place, the width of Oxford Street. The intention from the outset was to provide landscaped streets, instead of more corporate squares and piazzas. Deciduous trees and grasses and plants embrace the seasonal nature of the British climate.

14

15

maximum interior flexibility by locating columns off the planning grid so walls can always be taken past the columns.

Both inside and outside the new buildings, artists are collaborating with the architects on a public art programme that, although not yet on the scale of that for Broadcasting House, looks set to ensure that the BBC media campus will be a far cry from a corporate business park. Isabel Vasseur and Rebecca Ward of Art Project Management produced a public art strategy document for the BBC in 2001. The team at Broadcasting House was obliged to implement a public art programme by Westminster City Council, but at White City no such obligation existed. Art Project Management's document argued that 'the site needs to have a vibrant identity in what is currently an indifferent suburban location. Equally, the staff of the BBC deserve an environment which reflects their own creativity and if the Per Cent for Art policy is adopted the local community will enjoy a new and exciting destination.' The results of the proposal are shown in Chapter 9.

As this book goes to press, construction is already six months ahead of schedule. But even before completion of this phase a shortlist has been announced for a further architectural competition – this time for a music centre and additional office accommodation to the south of Allies and Morrison's current building site. The star-studded list comprises Foreign Office Architects (London), Future Systems (London), MVRDV (Netherlands), Ushida Findlay Architects (London/Tokyo) and Zaha Hadid (London). The BBC is delivering on its promises and it looks certain that White City will, without doubt, become as exciting and dynamic a place to work and visit as its sister in the West End.

15 Computer image of interior of the entrance to the Broadcast Centre.

16 Computer image of interior view of the Central Office Building. A nautical image is expressed by the timber panels of the more enclosed offices, docking into the opposite, open façade which is reached by stairs with a gradual gradient.

16

17

17+18 Bovis Lend Lease on site during the summer of 2002. Although appointed by the BBC, Allies and Morrison's client is now Bovis Lend Lease who in turn is working for Land Securities Trillium, the BBC's property partner.

18

19

19 The foyer of the Broadcast Centre and Energy Centre, with the original building on the right, lit for a Christmas event to thank the project team, December 2002.

7

PACIFIC QUAY

14

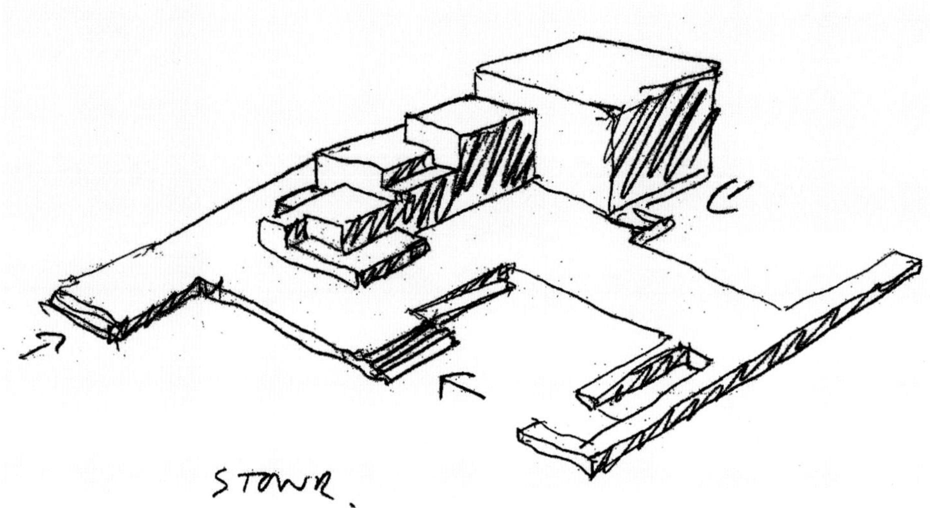

14-16 Sketches by David Chipperfield which show the tiered sequence of platforms and terraces which appear like a giant staircase. Its profile makes legible the division of public and private space. In section the building is a graphic representation of the process of broadcast production, from the studios at the base to the satellite farm on the roof.

15

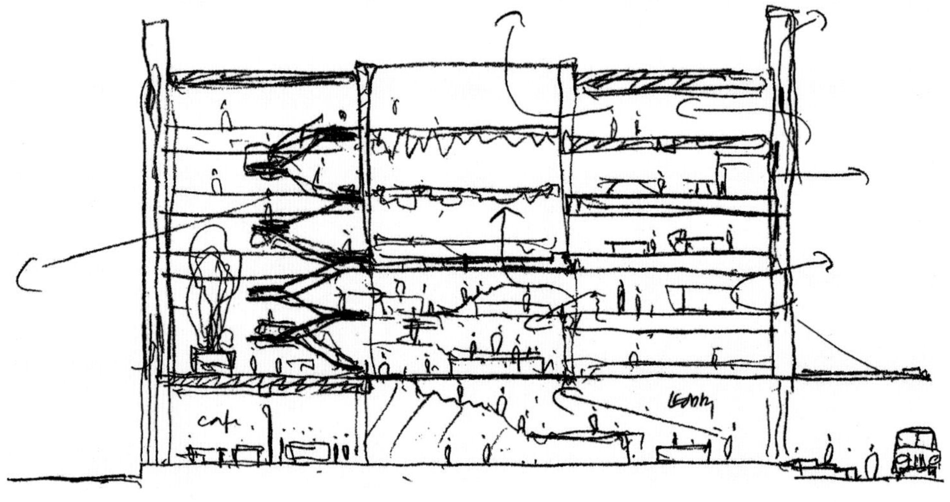

16

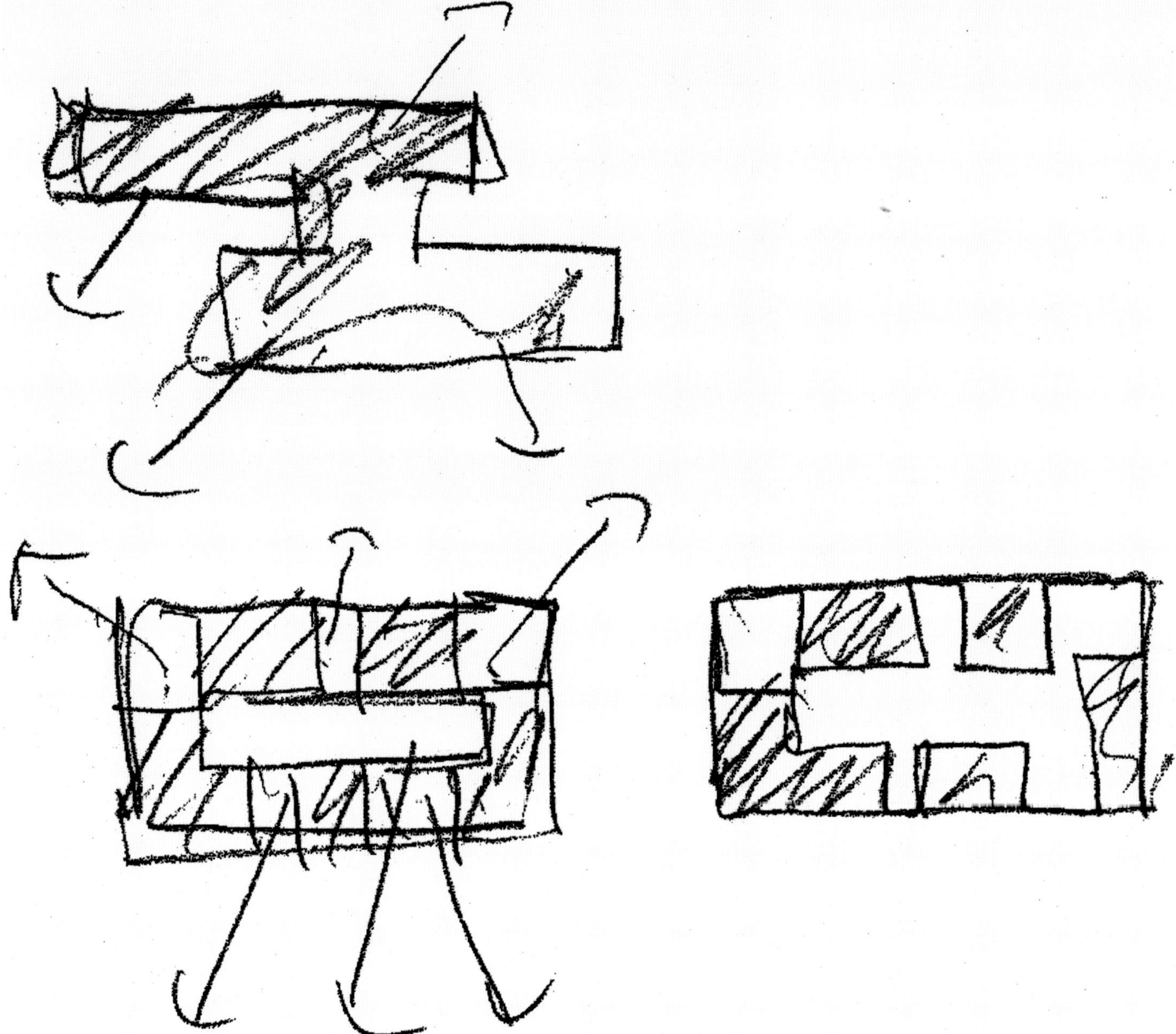

17 Model of the building without the double-glass skin which encloses it.

18 Ground floor plan.

19 First floor plan.

20 Second floor plan.

21 Third floor plan.

17

possibility of having individual control of windows and lighting, and team 'territories' with flexible boundaries. Chipperfield's office will be responsible for all the interiors and much of the furniture design for the building, which will house up to 1200 staff.

The new headquarters had to establish its own identity and has done so to stunning effect. The robust self-contained structure will not look incongruous standing alongside the currently abandoned Govan graving docks against a backdrop of the Kilpatrick Hills to the north. Yet it is also an elegant design of the refinement you would expect from Chipperfield's office. It will glow like a lantern at night and enable visitors and residents of the city to read the activity in the building. Through the double-skin glass walls, a tiered sequence of platforms and terraces appear like a giant staircase, under which are housed the studios. Its profile makes legible the division of public and private space: informal meeting areas are set out above the studios and the staircase encourages circulation and communication between departments. In section the building is a graphic representation of the process of broadcast production, from the studios at the base to the satellite farm on the roof.

On entering the building, visitors will immediately be aware of the grand sweep of public space from the 6 metre high reception. There will be a café and a BBC shop in this space, alongside the audience-handling area. This will also be the meeting point for tours of the building. Casual visitors to the public space will be able to access virtual guides to the building and programme-making activities. The architectural trick is to make the public feel as though they are gaining privileged access to their BBC, bringing them deep into the building without disrupting the daily business of the broadcasters or posing a security risk. The architect had to 'address the issue of making a public building without a public programme'.

Chipperfield says the most immediate formal problem lay 'in the compositional relationship between technical elements such as studios, that had to be solid, and office space, which in order to enjoy the surrounding views, had to be transparent'. The most difficult problem was the juxtaposition of the four-storey principal television studio (Studio A) and the adjoining office spaces. A design priority has been to ensure integration of facilities and common spaces, including technical areas, so that nowhere is relegated to 'back room' status. Two parallel bars of office space are arranged to maximise views within and without

18

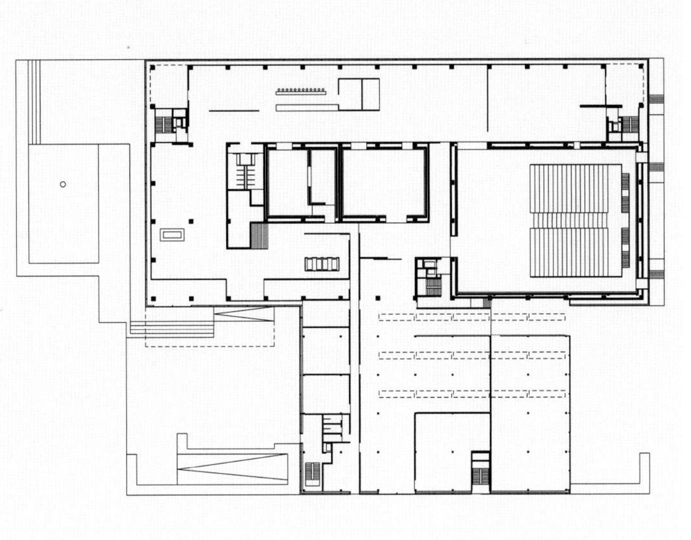

19

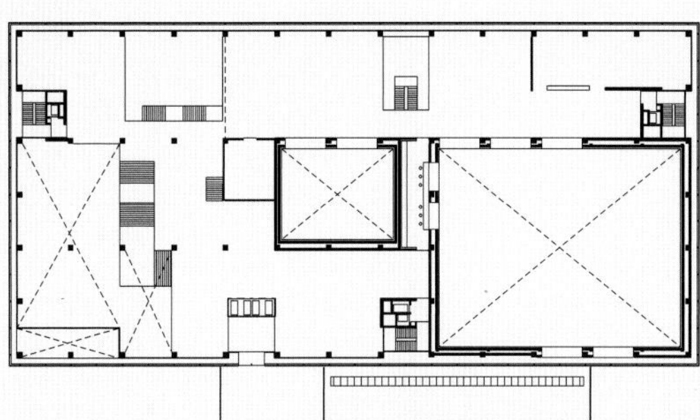

20

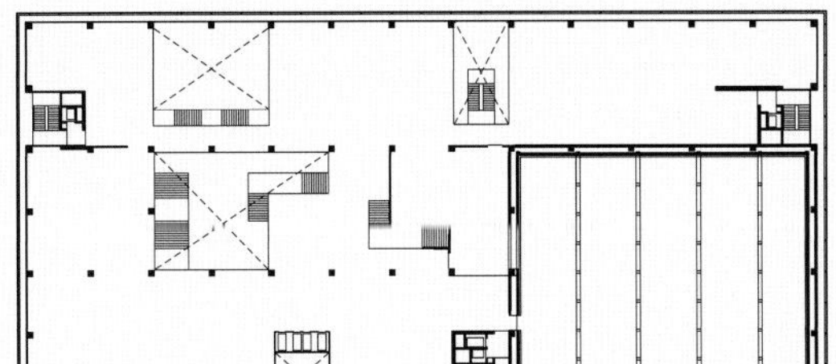

21

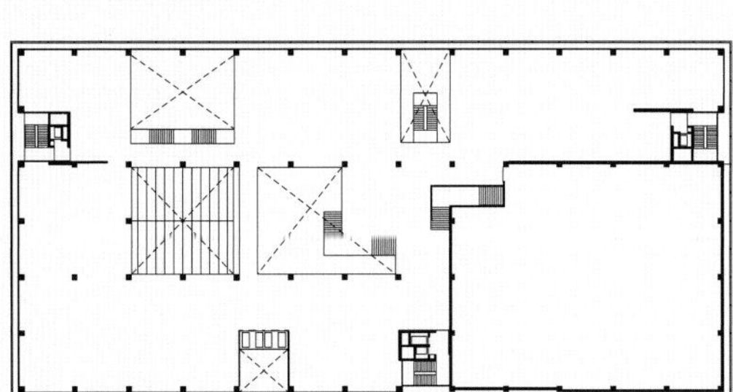

23

22 Computer image of the new BBC Scotland headquarters on completion. What looks like a glass box is in fact grounded on a solid base of sandstone slabs. Sandstone will be used throughout the building to define the semi-public route and connect the external and internal spaces.

BC Scotland

23

the building and provide flexibility and any combination of cellular, team or open-plan organisation. The double skin of the facade, with a fixed outer layer and opening inside layer, allows for natural ventilation while providing protection from wind and rain.

Although the drawings and model of Pacific Quay give the impression of a glass box, it is in fact grounded on a solid base that will be made from sandstone slabs. The vertical surfaces will be sandblasted; the horizontal surfaces will be polished and acid-etched. Sandstone will be used throughout the building to define the semi-public route and connect the external and internal spaces. The new BBC Scotland headquarters will be an architectural essay in contrasts: of the heavy staircase and light, airy public space and of the solid sandstone base and transparent glazed facade. It will be a hive of concentrated activity, much of which will be on view to the public but which will also accommodate the often private and intense business of making programmes. How quickly others will follow the BBC onto this exposed plot of land remains to be seen. Assuming the construction of a new bridge over the Clyde is given the go-ahead, access to the site should become relatively easy. It is the job of Chipperfield's building to inspire Glaswegians with a vibrant new place to work, and to provide the catalyst for a thoughtful redevelopment of the area so that, when the BBC's employees and visitors leave this self-contained architectural gem, they are not greeted by a cold blast of reality.

23 Computer image of the BBC building alongside the Glasgow Science Centre as seen from the opposite bank of the River Clyde.

24+25 BBC Scotland's 6m-high reception will be open and transparent. The focus will be the tiered sequence of platforms and terraces which will appear like a giant staircase, under which the studios are housed. There will be a café and a BBC shop in reception and it will function as the audience-handling area.

24

25

26

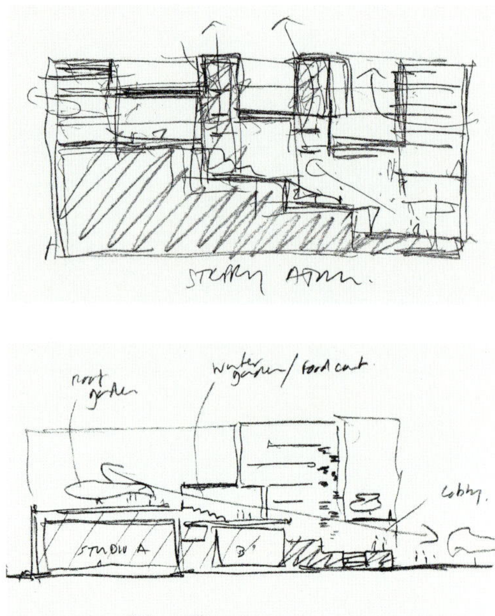

26 The platforms and terraces in the centre of the building will provide impromptu as well as more formal meeting places. The grand sweep of this central space also allows the visiting public to see right into the workings of BBC Scotland.

8

THE HEART OF THE COMMUNITY

2

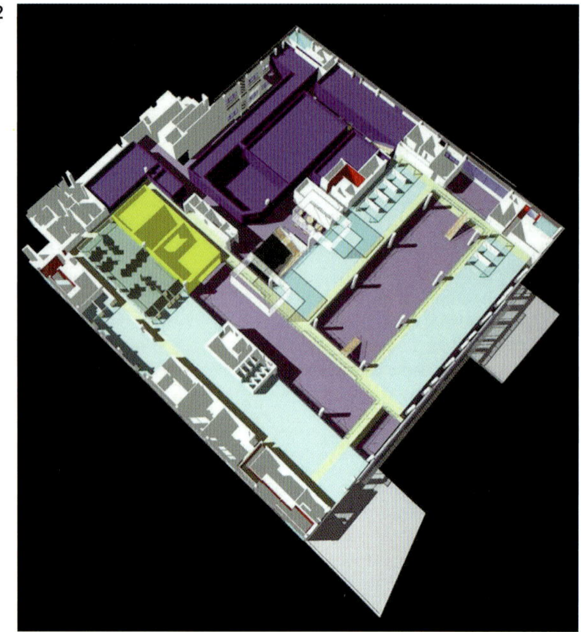

3

2 Computer image of the BBC's accommodation in The Mailbox, designed by The Building Design Partnership.

3 The BBC in Birmingham will soon be on the move from Pebble Mill. Shown here a computer image of The Mailbox, a high profile redevelopment of an old Royal Mail sorting office. The BBC will move in as one of the key tenants in 2004. A large new picture window on the canal-side of the building provides employees with a great view of the piazza.

4 The Mailbox is the focus of the regeneration of Brimingham's city centre. It will provide the BBC with a shop-front in the heart of Birmingham, in contrast to the campus at Pebble Mill.

Rather than building on a new site, the BBC opted to become a tenant of The Mailbox, a high-profile redevelopment of an old Royal Mail sorting office and the focus of the regeneration of Birmingham's city centre. The BBC's accommodation has generous floor plates and ceiling heights, allowing for the insertion of mezzanine levels without compromising the volume of the interior spaces. A large new picture window on the canal-side of the building will give employees a fantastic view over the piazza. The front overlooks the central street of The Mailbox development, giving the BBC a shop-front in the heart of Birmingham. The BBC's architect is Building Design Partnership, which is working with IDEA on interior design, space planning and theming. David George, the BBC's Project Director for The Mailbox, enthuses about 'the opportunities presented by more flexible space for team-working and communicating' in a way that was not possible at Pebble Mill. The success of the move will be tested when the BBC moves in January 2004.

Similarly, in Norwich, the BBC has taken space in a new architectural landmark: the Forum, designed by Michael Hopkins and Partners. Although the BBC's current base is only minutes away from the Forum, at All Saints Green, it feels more suburban and removed from the heart of the market town's medieval centre. Radio is housed on the ground floor of a 10-storey tower, with television in the building across the street. The move to the Forum in the summer of 2003 will integrate radio and television and heighten the public's awareness of the BBC. Its bid for tenancy has presented some problems, largely to do with the fact that the building contract was already underway. The intention was to design an

4

5

6

auditorium and bar in the space now taken by the BBC. It was too late to alter the shell of the building but, as project architect Laura Carrara Cagni explains: 'We made all the effort we could inside because we believed the BBC was the right tenant for the building.' That effort has involved a certain amount of compromise, but all the necessary office and studio space has been accommodated – much of which overlooks the Forum and the atrium. The bar and canteen, which was requested by the BBC, has not materialised yet one can't help feeling that this is a good thing. The point about the Forum, which houses the city library as well as several shops and restaurants, is that all tenants should use the facilities in and around the building, making it a true 'civic institution' as intended by the city and county councils. They wanted a landmark suitable for the new millennium, 'a centre of knowledge, information and learning'. The BBC is, of course, a perfect fit and will add dynamism and vitality to the place, particularly if the occasional radio or television programme is transmitted from within the atrium.

The BBC is keen to associate itself with other regional cultural institutions, and even form partnerships, as it has done in Leeds. The existing Leeds building, which is in fact three buildings knocked into one, has never been used efficiently. It was not deemed financially expedient to redevelop it, and a new site was sought that would offer more open-plan working. During the search, the team heard that the Leeds College of Music was looking for a partner with whom to develop a new auditorium. An agreement was reached with developer Rushbond Properties, whereby the BBC and the college would become joint tenants of a new building in the emerging

5-7 Computer images of the interior of the BBC's accommodation in The Mailbox. Generous floor-plates and ceiling heights allow for the insertion of mezzanine levels without compromising on the volume of the space.

7

Quarry Hill arts quarter of the city centre. The BBC's new regional headquarters will fill the ground, first and second floors, with the college's auditorium on the third floor. The BBC will benefit enormously from its site adjacent to the West Yorkshire Playhouse and Leeds College of Music and opposite a dance school. Plans are already afoot for Radio 3 concerts in the new auditorium. The building is designed by DLA Architecture, formerly David Lyons Associates, with some input from the BBC. The BBC is responsible for its own fit-out.

Occasionally, the association is not with a cultural institution but with a watering hole. When the BBC was looking for a new property in Hull, it heard about the redevelopment of Portcullis House in the city centre, also by DLA Architecture. The original building was being ripped down by the developer, Manor Properties, with the intention of replacing it with apartments and a pub. What was going to be the pub, on the corner of the new building, is now going to be occupied by the BBC (from ground to second floor). It's a far cry from the current building; an old army recruitment centre above the post office in Chapel Street where the facilities for staff are poor and the reception area is cramped and uninviting. The new building is right in the centre of Hull, opposite the Queen's Gardens Fountain in the main shopping district.

In some cases relocation is considered for strategic reasons – not simply because the facilities are outdated or the building isolated. In Kent, the BBC was looking to create a new television base as part of its strategy to improve the local nature of the regional news. The new home was found in the Great Hall at Tunbridge Wells, which is ideally located for Kent and East Sussex. To achieve the bi-media ideal, the local radio station was moved from Chatham into the same space. A small base has been kept in the original building in Chatham to serve the Medway area. The outside of the building, while impressive, is neither modern nor dramatic, but it fits the bill by being central, open and inviting to the public. Situated minutes from the railway station, the Great Hall is on the edge of the retail area in the city centre and has an arcade running through the middle of it. It was refurbished after a fire gutted it 15 years ago and housed offices for a building society and Waterstone's bookshop. The BBC acquired separate leases and took them all, subletting the second floor.

As well as reconsidering the location of many of the regional stations, the BBC has been looking at other ways in which it can assert its presence within the community.

8 Ground floor plan of the Forum in Norwich by Michael Hopkins and Partners.
Key:
1 Square
2 Forum
3 Library
4 Tourist information centre
5 Origins
6 Café

9 The BBC was keen to move into the heart of the market town's medieval centre, even though its current base is only minutes away. The primary tenant is the library, replacing the central library which burnt down in 1994. The building contract was already underway when the BBC bid for tenancy. Although the shell could not be altered the necessary office and studio space has been accommodated, with much of it overlooking the Forum and the atrium.

8

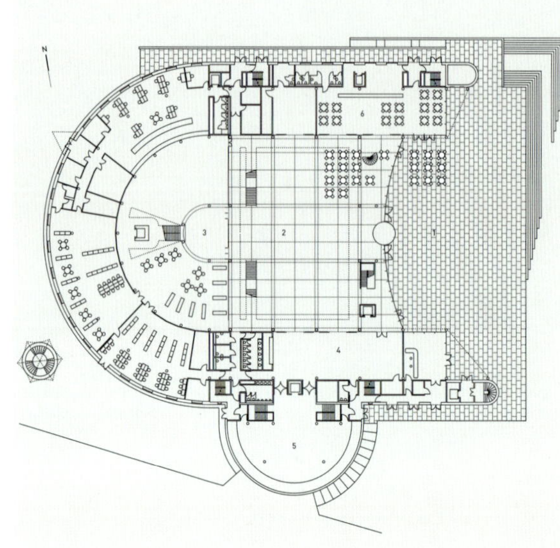

9

Sylvia Hines, Head of New Services, Nations and Regions, tells an amusing story of an early visit to BBC Hull. The original building, despite its central location is, as outlined above, 'very grotty'. She was sitting in reception when a local came rushing in clutching a tape. 'I've got a cassette here', she said 'please can you copy it for me?' The receptionist, despite being slightly taken aback by the request, saw no reason why she shouldn't carry out this simple task for a loyal listener. The point Hines is making is that 'it is usually despite the condition of the buildings, and more because of the quality of the output' that the local radio stations around the country foster such a feeling of ownership and belonging among the audiences. How much stronger that will be when more of the buildings are obviously accessible to those audiences, as is the plan.

Hines is convinced that the strategy will have a big impact and says that it is the desire to extend the connection of local stations to new audiences, beyond the traditional 55+ age category, that has inspired the creation of new Open Centres around the country. 'We were aware that we should be making space more accessible to people, but the idea was sharpened when Greg Dyke became Director-General.' Engagement with the community and promoting local diversity has always been high on his agenda. As ITV centralises, the local aspect of the BBC's coverage becomes increasingly important.

The Capital Modernisation Fund was set up by the Government's Department for Education and Skills with the aim of giving everyone access to the internet. This was relevant to the BBC because of the amount of investment it is putting into its portfolio of websites. So it applied to the fund for cash to part-finance

10

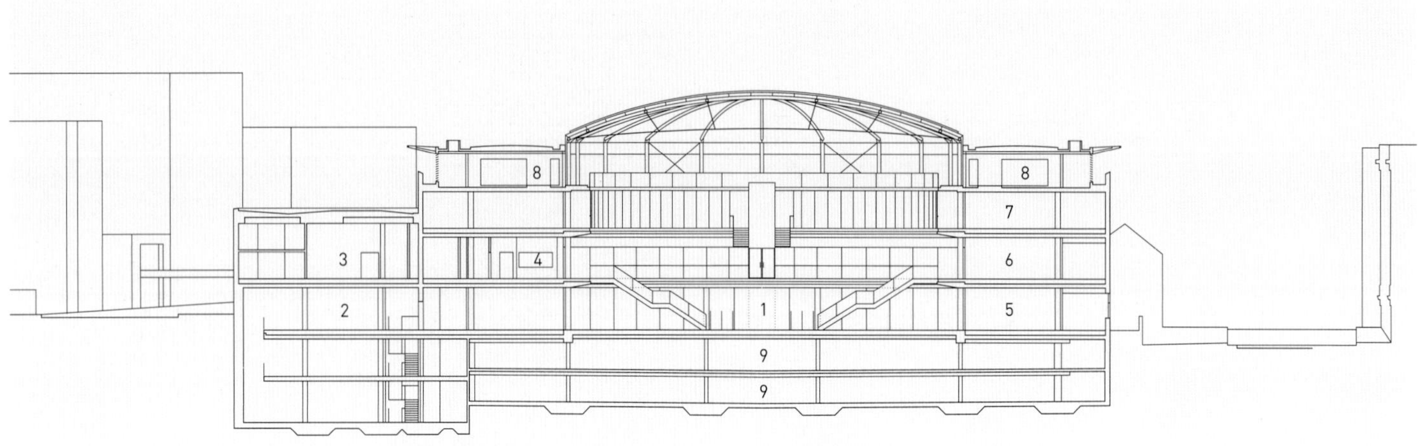

Learning Centres that provide free access to computers and make tutors available on site. The BBC set up partnerships with local lifelong learning providers who pay for the tutors. Most of the centres are open to everyone at all times, but some also run specialist courses that must be booked in advance. The important thing, stresses Hines, is that the content of the courses 'should be linked to the BBC's output on the whole, otherwise they sit as an odd adjunct. At Stoke we set up a partnership with the WRVC and a local hostel for the homeless. The people doing the makeover are using the BBC Learning Centre where they access the BBC's "How to be a gardener" website and in the process learn computer as well as gardening skills. The makeover of the hostel is being followed on local radio and students are making a video which will be edited for use on regional television.'

There are currently five Open Centres in Blackburn, Sheffield, Merseyside (Liverpool), Stoke and Brighton. They are all in central locations and tend to be in smaller cities where they are filling an information gap and providing an even more valuable service. The spread also reflects an increase in the BBC's investment in the North of England. Brighton is an exception in more ways than just location. Its centre, although in the BBC building, is run by Community Service Volunteers and offers longer-term courses only.

In much smaller centres around the country, the BBC is reaching out beyond its buildings. Buses with publicly accessible computers at one end and a broadcast area at the other travel to places where, as one member of the public put it, 'only the cops ever show up'. It is in these districts, and in cities across the country, that the BBC excels. 'Good local broadcasting nurtures and consolidates the self esteem of local communities,' says Pat Loughrey. Good buildings are the vital interface between the broadcasters and those communities.

10 Section through the Forum.

Key:

1 Atrium

2 Origins

3 BBC TV studio

4 BBC Radio studio

5 Catering

6 Retail unit

7 Library stacks

8 Plant

9 Car park

11 Interior view with the library in the foreground.

12 The 15th century church of St Peter's Mancroft reflected in the glazed entrance to the Forum.

12

11

13

13 Night view of the Forum. The building was completed in 2001 and the BBC will move in during the summer of 2003.

9

PUBLIC ART

10 Detail of winning proposal by Tony Cooper/ Martin Richman for permanent lighting scheme. Computer generated image indicating LED 'network' in the curved façade of the new BH. Image © 2002 Tony Cooper

11 Painting by Martin Richman to indicate lighting concept for BH by Tony Cooper/ Martin Richman. Image © 2002 Martin Richman

10

MacCormac endorses her comment, and describes the Broadcasting House site as an interstitial space, or shoreline, between the two distinct urban characters; the noisy bustle of retail in Oxford Circus and Regent Street, and the more restrained Portland Place, occupied by almost-silent institutions.

Abigail Appleton, head of speech radio for Radio 3, sees no reason why radio shouldn't be regarded as 'art in its own right'. Radio 3 has been commissioning work throughout its history, and the producers of the programmes are often 'artists'. Recently, the station commissioned a sound composition by the artist Tacita Dean for a programme *Between the Ears*. 'This is an example of how adventurous broadcasters can be. We should think about commissioning art that can work as a broadcast too – we should focus on complementary commissioning.'

11

Appleton's presentation at the workshop was greeted with unanimous approval and respect. It seems likely that we will see, or rather hear, some impressive work as part of the new 'BBC experience'.

How is the art being commissioned?
Vivien Lovell and Louise Trodden started to research artists specifically for the BH public art programme from the end of October 2001, adding to their extensive database of artists. Lovell uncovered new ideas and artists while travelling in Japan, the USA and Europe, and research is ongoing. 'With a long-term programme like this, you can't commission all the artists at the same time – a commissions framework and action plan for priority commissions is agreed, and inevitably the results of one competition

20

21

existing and future work. It would seem that in the excitement of considering future collaborations and commissions, the BBC has woken up to the need to catalogue and evaluate its collection.

The BBC is one of the most important and influential patrons of the arts in this country, investing as much as the Arts Council in new work each year. As MacCormac sees it, the public art programme 'is just an extension of the transaction with the public that the BBC has. The public is a highly critical receiver', and will soon voice opinions on the success or otherwise of the BBC's choice of artists at Broadcasting House and White City. 'The project's sustainability depends on its adaptability', he says of Broadcasting House. 'I think we need a loose-fit concept. BBC Experience was a tight-fit concept which didn't work. All this needs is clever interpretation.'

That's probably right. But a combination of reasonably tightly curated formal work, and more informal commissioning will only further the overall success of the programme, each acting as a foil for the other. It remains to be seen who will have long-term curatorial responsibility for the art programme and art collection once Broadcasting House opens. However, if the enthusiasm within the BBC remains as infectious and deep-rooted as it is today, it is not unreasonable to predict the ground-breaking success of this – and all the other – current building-related public art projects by the BBC.

20+21 The giant mural by John Piper and the fountain by TB Huxley Jones were two works of art commissioned for Television Centre when it first opened.

22 Thomas Cox-Bisham "play", 2002. A sticky-tape dragon created by the artist and children of Canberra Primary School as an exercise in building the ideal playground.

22

23

23 'On foot' – a walk along Great Portland Street filmed by pupils of the Gateway Primary School, Westminster, edited by Ruth Maclennan and Richard Wentworth. Video still, 2003. Project organised with Modus Operandi and the 21CC.

Broadcasting House
Architectural competition jury
Director, Network Radio: Jenny Abramsky
Chairman BBC Governors:
Sir Christopher Bland
Director, Cities Programme, London School
of Economics: Ricky Burdett
Director, World Service: Mark Byford
Director-General: Greg Dyke
Director, News: Tony Hall
Chairman, Commission for Architecture and
the Built Environment (CABE): Sir Stuart Lipton
Director, Property – Facilitator: Ian Robertson
Director, Finance, Property and Business Affairs:
John Smith
Director, Drama, Entertainment, Children's: Alan Yentob

Project team
BBC Project Director: Chris Evans
BBC Programme Manager: Joanna Streeten
Project Manager: Bob Ogilvie
Architects: MacCormac, Jamieson, Prichard
Contractor: Bovis Lend Lease
Art Consultant: Modus Operandi
Structural Engineers: Whitby Bird
Mechanical and Electrical Contractors: Faber Maunsell
Cost Consultants: Currie and Brown
Planning Team: Andrew Fullerton (BBC);
Nathaniel Lichfield: Linklaters, Urban Initiatives,

White City
Architectural competition jury
Head of Finance, Broadcast: Alan Bancroft
Chairman: Sir Christopher Bland
Director Cities Programme, London School
of Economics: Ricky Burdett
Chairman, Commission for Architecture and
the Built Environment (CABE): Sir Stuart Lipton
Director, Broadcasting: Pam Masters
Broadcast Project, Project Director: Peter Siggins
Director, Finance, Property and Business Affairs:
John Smith
Director Drama, Entertainment, Children's: Alan Yentob

Project team
BBC Project Director: Tony Wilson
BBC Development Manager: Roger Ackroyd
Project Manager/Cost Consultant: Gleeds
Project Management, Property Development and
Facilities Management:Land Securities Trillium
Architects: Allies and Morrison
Interior Design: DEGW
Landscape Design: Christopher Bradley-Hole
Contractor: Bovis Lend Lease
Art Consultant: Art Project Management
Mechanical and Electrical Contractors/
Structural Engineers: Buro Happold

Pacific Quay
Architectural competition jury
Land Securities: John Andersen
Director, Cities Programme, London School
of Economics: Ricky Burdett
Director-General: Greg Dyke
REEF Property Investment: David Hunter
Barcelona planner: David Mackay
Head of Programmes, BBC Scotland: Ken MacQuarrie
Controller Scotland: John McCormick
Creative Director Arts and Factual, BBC Scotland:
May Miller
Mackintosh School of Art and Design, Glasgow:
Professor David Porter
Director, Property: Ian Robertson
Director, Finance, Property and Business Affairs:
John Smith
Scottish Governor: Sir Robert Smith
Editor, Domus; Director, Glasgow City of Culture 1999:
Deyan Sudjic

Project team
BBC Project Director: Iain Marley
BBC Development Manager: Mark Swindlehurst
Architects: David Chipperfield Architects

Credits
Greg Dyke, Director-General, BBC; **John Smith,** Director, Finance, Property and Business Affairs, BBC; **Alan Yentob,** Director, Drama, Entertainment and CBBC; **Pat Loughrey,** Director of Nations and Regions, BBC; **Ian Robertson,** Director of Property, BBC; **John McCormick,** Controller, BBC Scotland; **John Dee,** Head of Interior Design, BBC Property

With special thanks to: Leonora Thomson; Guy Saich; John Dee; George Crowe; Ken Cargill; Lucy Jones; Joanna Bacon; Hau Ming Tse; Ian Small; Concetta Sidoti; Jeff Walden (BBC Archive, Caversham).

Selected bibliography
History of BBC Broadcasting House by Guy Saich, 2001; *History of BBC Television Centre* by Guy Saich, 2001; *The Architectural Review*, August 1932; *The Architectural Review*, May 1987; *Modern Wireless*, March 1931; *Broadcasting House Heritage Study* by Mike Evans and Mark Hines, MJP; *Broadcasting House*, The British Broadcasting Corporation, 1932, Curwen Press, Plaistow.

Picture credits
ITN HQ – Nigel Young/Foster and Partners, Channel 4 HQ – Richard Bryant/Arcaid, Paul McGill, Tully Chaudry, Ed Miller. BBC Photo Library; **Allies and Morrison,** Miller Hare, Kandor/Andrew Putnam; **David Chipperfield Architects,** Richard Davies; **MacCormac Jamieson Prichard,** Niamh Billings models, Nick Grace, Robbie Polley, Hayes Davidson, Virtual Artworks;

Designed and produced by Wordsearch

Index

Alexandra Palace 74, 78, 80
All Souls Church 6, 14, 37, 40, 63
Allan Murray Architects 111
Allies and Morrison 17, 88-106, 148
Alsop & Stormer 53
Architectural Review, The 10, 23, 26, 36
Art Project Management 102, 148, 151
Arup Associates 34
BBC regions124-133
Birt, John 13, 16, 44, 50, 88
Bland, Christopher 44, 82
Bovis Lend Lease 98
Bradley-Hole, Christopher 94, 95, 148
Broadcasting House 10, 12, 14, 17, 20-31, 34, 37, 44, 48-73, 74, 78, 80, 84, 88, 90, 92, 99, 102, 111, 124, 136-152
Building Design Partnership 126
Burdett, Ricky 6-8, 16, 52, 90, 110
Bush House 88
Capital Radio 15
Cargill, Ken 112
Cayford, Paul 151
Chermayeff, Serge 26, 48, 136
Chipperfield, David 7, 17, 44, 110
Coates, Wells 26, 48, 136
Cotton, Bill 82
Cox-Bisham, Thomas 151
Crowe, George 44, 88
Daily Express, The 30
David Chipperfield Architects 108-120
Dawbarn, Graham 12, 74, 78, 82
Dee, John 50
DEGW 50, 52, 84, 99, 148
DLA Architecture 129
Dyke, Greg 14, 16, 44, 53, 84, 88, 108, 124, 130
Egton House 14, 58
Electrophone Company, The 20
Ellerman, Sir John 23
Eric Parry Architects 53
Evans, Chris 52, 53, 84, 142
Fletcher Priest 53
Foley House 37
Fontana, Bill 149
Forum (Norwich) 126, 128
Foster and Partners 34-45
Foster, Norman 10, 17
Francis, Dick 36, 44
Franco British Exhibition 76-78
Fullerton, Andrew 53
Furlong, William 147
George, David 126
Gill, Eric 28, 136, 149
Goldsmith, Commander VH 26
Hall, Tony 13, 88
Head, Tim 148
Hines, Mark 56
Hines, Sylvia 130, 132
Howard, George 42, 44, 88
Huxley, Paul 151
Huxley-Jones, TB 80,136
Ian Ritchie Architects 90
IDEA 126
James, Alan 42, 90
Jaray, Tess 151
John McAslan and Partners 90
Keating, Roly 13, 17
Kirk, Bruce 148
Koetter Kim & Associates 112
Kossoff, Leon 151
Land Securities Trillium 15, 17, 98, 99
Langham Hotel 22, 34, 37
Langham Place 34, 37, 40, 44, 88, 110
Langham Street 14, 23, 58, 62, 63, 36, 142
Larsen, Nikolaj 151
Lime Grove 13, 78, 82
Lipton, Sir Stuart 15, 16, 52, 90, 92, 39
Listener, The 28
Llewelyn Davies 52
Long, Richard 151
Loughrey, Pat 124, 132
Lovell, Vivien 136-152
MacCormac Jamieson Prichard 10, 17, 26, 34, 48-72, 147
MacCormac, Sir Richard 17, 30, 48-72, 138, 139, 143, 152
Mackintosh, Charles Rennie 108, 110
Mailbox (Birmingham) 14, 126
Marconi House 26
Marley, Ian 110
McCormick, John 112
McGrath, Raymond 26, 48
Mecanoo Architecten 111
Michael Hopkins and Partners 126
Modern Wireless, The 25
Modus Operandi 136-152
Orwell, George 66
Pacific Quay 10, 17, 44, 106-122
Page and Park Architects 111
Pebble Mill 124
Pei, I.M 34
Piper, John 136
Portland Place 10, 13, 22, 23, 25, 26, 28, 30, 37, 62, 63, 136, 144
Queen Margaret Drive 108, 110
Reith, John 20, 24, 26, 28, 45, 74
Riverside Studios, Hammersmith 78
RMJM 90
Robertson, Ian 5, 16, 90, 110
Roche, Kevin 34
Rogers, Richard 34, 111
Sauerbruch Hutton 111
Saugier, Bertrand 149
Savoy Hill 20, 26
Scott, Brownrigg Turner 44, 88
Shiraishi, Yuko 150, 151
Smith, John 14-17, 34, 40, 44, 53, 84, 88, 90, 92
Stanton Williams 53
Streeten, Joanna 52
Television Centre 12-14, 36, 42, 48, 74-86, 90, 136
Terry Farrell and Partners 34
Thivillon, Pascal 150
Tudsbery, Marmaduke T.10, 22, 24, 52, 78, 80
Val Myer, Lieutenant-Colonel G.10, 20, 22, 23, 24, 26, 48, 52, 62, 78
Vasseur, Isabel 102, 148, 151
Wentworth, Richard 136, 141, 146
White City 10, 14, 15, 17, 20, 42, 44, 48, 52, 62, 76, 78, 87-106, 124, 136, 146, 148-152
Wilkinson Eyre Architects 111
Wilson, Tony 92
Wright, Elizabeth 148
Yass, Catherine 146
Yentob, Alan 16, 17, 44, 53, 56, 84, 136, 150
Young, Stuart 42, 45, 88